David Metzger Library
Nazareth College
Kalamazoo, Michigan 49074

PROPERTY OF
BAKER COLLEGE
Owosso Campus

D1287843

PR
BAKER
Owosso Cam

SOUTHERN LITERARY STUDIES

## SOUTHERN LITERARY STUDIES
Louis D. Rubin, Jr., Editor

*A Season of Dreams: The Fiction of Eudora Welty*
ALFRED APPEL, JR.

*The Hero with the Private Parts*
ANDREW LYTLE

*Hunting in the Old South: Original Narratives of the Hunters*
EDITED BY CLARENCE GOHDES

*Joel Chandler Harris: A Biography*
PAUL M. COUSINS

*John Crowe Ransom: Critical Essays and a Bibliography*
EDITED BY THOMAS DANIEL YOUNG

*A Bibliographical Guide to the Study of Southern Literature*
EDITED BY LOUIS D. RUBIN, JR.

*Poe: Journalist and Critic*
ROBERT D. JACOBS

*Love, Boy: The Letters of Mac Hyman*
EDITED BY WILLIAM BLACKBURN

*The Complete Works of Kate Chopin*
EDITED BY PER SEYERSTED

*Kate Chopin: A Critical Biography*
PER SEYERSTED

*Without Shelter: The Early Career of Ellen Glasgow*
J. R. RAPER

*Southern Excursions: Essays on Mark Twain and Others*
LEWIS LEARY

*The Poetry of Randall Jarrell*
SUZANNE FERGUSON

*Death by Melancholy: Essays on Modern Southern Fiction*
WALTER SULLIVAN

*The Sovereign Wayfarer: Walker Percy's Diagnosis of the Malaise*
MARTIN LUSCHEI

*Literature and Society in Early Virginia, 1608–1840*
RICHARD BEALE DAVIS

*The Question of Flannery O'Connor*
MARTHA STEPHENS

*Grace King of New Orleans: A Selection of Her Writings*
EDITED BY ROBERT BUSH

The Question of Flannery O'Connor

# The Question of

# Flannery O'Connor

MARTHA STEPHENS

Louisiana State University Press
Baton Rouge

PROPERTY OF
BAKER COLLEGE
Owosso C

ISBN 0–8071–0000–5
Library of Congress Catalog Card Number 73–77656
Copyright © 1973 by Louisiana State University Press
All rights reserved
Manufactured in the United States of America
Printed by The Colonial Press Inc., Clinton, Massachusetts
Designed by Albert Crochet

813.54
St 11

# Contents

65334

**David Metzger Library**
Nazareth College
Kalamazoo, Michigan 49074

# Acknowledgments

Many people have given me help and support in the writing of this book; I can mention only a few. I am grateful to Lois Logan, for secretarial and editorial help of unusual perspicuity; to the University of Cincinnati for two special grants which gave me time to complete the book; to Louis Rubin, for good advice on an early draft; to Melvin J. Friedman and Lewis A. Lawson, for the excellent aids to O'Connor study in their compendium *The Added Dimension* (Fordham University Press, 1966); to Robert Drake, for his important early essay *Flannery O'Connor* (William B. Eerdmans, 1966); to my husband, Jerone Stephens, for making it possible, indeed necessary, for me to write; to my children, Daniel, Paige, and Shelley, for occasional forbearance (and so that they will at least get to see their names in print); and to their courageous nursemaids, Doris Harris, Octavia Patman, and Shirley Netter.

The Question of Flannery O'Connor

# Chapter I

# Belief and the Tonal Dimension

Flannery O'Connor is not likely to prove, in the long run, an easy writer to assess; and it may well be that many a future chronicler of American letters, poised on the edge of an O'Connor judgment, will find himself much vexed. This is not to say that there is not considerable unanimity about O'Connor at the present time—one reads and hears a great many expressions of happily uncomplicated admiration. Even so, it would seem that the more interesting appraisals are coming, as they have come all along, since the earliest reviews of *Wise Blood,* from those who have deeply ambivalent feelings to express about this writer, and it may be that as more and more readers come to know and to react to the body of her work as a whole, this ambivalence will be felt more widely.

In O'Connor's case, one has to be particularly suspicious of the platitudinous phrase of approval. That she was a gifted writer—astonishingly good at times—certainly no one wishes to dispute; but the fact is that she was possessed of so eccentric, at times so—we must face this to begin with—repugnant a view of human life that the strain of trying to enter emotionally into her work is often very great indeed. No one was more conscious of this problem than she herself; she was very much aware of facing an audience essentially hostile to her assumptions about human life, and she did not expect—nor, one sometimes thinks, did she even desire—easy acceptance from it. She said that what she wanted to do was to restore the reader's "sense of evil," and she obviously did not expect that he would wholly enjoy it.

The problem, then, in trying to make a balanced judgment about this writer is simple enough to state. O'Connor clearly had a great natural gift for the story-telling art—the better one knows her work, the more one comes to respect her ability. But she was also a highly doctrinal writer with a marked evangelical strain, and like all such writers—like D. H. Lawrence, for instance, and in France her fellow Catholics François Mauriac and Georges Bernanos—she poses so personal, so goading a challenge to a reader's perceptions of life that coming to terms with her as an artist is difficult.

To say that Miss O'Connor was a devout Catholic hardly begins to suggest how formidable the distance is between her view of life and the prevailing view of modern readers. To find so bleak, so austere and rigid, so other-worldly a Christian view of life as hers, one is forced back into the distant past of English religious literature—into the dark side of medieval Christian thought with its constant injunction to renunciation of the world. "All Christen people, biholde and see/ This world is but a vanytee"—her stories, like the twelfth-century verse, seem to enjoin us. How can it be, the O'Connor books seem to ask, that—in the words this time of the *Everyman* poet—"every man liveth so after their own pleasure and yet of their life they be nothing sure"? Let us beware, they urge, that it is not with us as it was with the evil ones in the time of Lot, for they too—in the words of Saint Luke—"did eat, they drank, they bought, they sold, they planted, they builded; But the same day that Lot went out of Sodom it rained fire and brimstone from heaven, and destroyed them all."

One must, of course, say *seem*—the stories *seem* to enjoin, to ask, to urge, for one does not wish to imply

that the O'Connor stories and novels are not wholly
dramatic. On the contrary, there is not a word of authorial argument as such. And yet the message and the warning are there; in story after story O'Connor sets up her
Sodom and brings it down, sets it up and brings it down.
Here the wretched Mrs. Mays, the Mrs. Copes, the Ray-
bers and Julians and Asburys suffer their terrible Christian comeuppance—foolish, deluded creatures who think
they possess something, know something, can achieve
something, who (as if, like brute animals, they have never
discovered the fact of their own mortality) take some
dumb pride in having reached a position of material or
emotional security. "I've seen them come, and I've seen
them go," says Mrs. McIntyre of her hired help, and we
know she's thinking, "But I'm here, I stay, I'm safe."
But of course no one is safe; eventually the fire and brimstone is rained down—O'Connor brings on, to wreak their
destruction, her mad bulls, her demonic children, her
escaped convicts. See, these stories seem to say, devastation, annihilation always around the corner, and yet the
godless go on acting as if they held their fates in their
own hands.

Of course the disasters that overtake these people, in
their blind struggle toward some foolish worldly end, are
not meant to seem gratuitous. They are presented, typically, as blessings in disguise, really as acts of grace; for
even if they are not fatal, they provide such violent
shocks to the characters' egos, to their sense of well-being,
that they are forced to see themselves (we are given to
understand) as they really are. And often enough, the
descent of grace, as it were, *is* fatal, as in the case of
Mrs. May in "Greenleaf." A veteran O'Connor reader
prepares himself for the worst when, midway through
this story, the smug Mrs. May, reacting to the taunts of
her sons, mutters, "They needn't think I'm going to die
any time soon . . . I'll die when I get good and ready."
We know that she is never going to get by with that, and

again a biblical line as it is echoed in *Everyman* springs
to mind: "O Death, thou camest when I had thee least in
mind!" And indeed when Mrs. May sees the bull racing
toward her, she cannot grasp, she cannot believe, what
is happening to her: she stands quite still, in a state not
of fright, but of "freezing unbelief":

> She stared at the violent black streak bounding toward her
> as if she had no sense of distance, as if she could not decide
> at once what his intention was, and the bull had buried his
> head in her lap, like a wild tormented lover, before her ex-
> pression changed. One of his horns sank until it pierced her
> heart and the other curved around her side and held her in
> an unbreakable grip. She continued to stare straight ahead
> but the entire scene in front of her had changed—the tree
> line was a dark wound in a world that was nothing but sky
> —and she had the look of a person whose sight had been
> suddenly restored but who finds the light unbearable.

More than this—of Mrs. May's death epiphany—we do
not know, except that as she sinks down over the bull's
head, she seems to be "whispering some last discovery
into the animal's ear." And yet the reader feels that he
must regard her as being radically changed, perhaps
"saved," by her violent death—as if for some people, so
set in their prideful, ungodly ways, it is only the ultimate
trauma of being separated from their bodies that can
induce them to see. Some such thing as this happens, apparently, to the grandmother in "A Good Man Is Hard to
Find," for when the Misfit shoots her he says, "She
would have been a good woman if there had been somebody there to shoot her every minute of her life."

The idea of death as a manifestation of grace, which
is central to a number of O'Connor works, is fully explained in a book by the Jesuit priest to whose writings
Miss O'Connor often paid her respects, Teilhard de Chardin. Describing, in *The Divine Milieu*, the soul's progress
toward the final leap out of itself which delivers it from
its own bondage into full union with the divine, Teilhard
writes that near the end of the "progressive breaking

down of our self-regard" we may still have the impression of "possessing ourselves in a supreme degree," for we will not yet have "crossed the critical point of our ex-centration, of our reversion to God."

> There is a further step to take: the one that makes us lose all foothold within ourselves. . . .
> In itself, death is an incurable weakness of corporeal beings, complicated, in our world, by the influence of an original fall. It is the sum and type of all the forces that diminish us, and against which we must fight without being able to hope for a personal, direct and immediate victory. Now the great victory of the Creator and Redeemer, in the Christian vision, is to have transformed what is in itself a universal power of diminishment and extinction into an essentially life-giving factor. God must, in some way or other, make room for himself, hollowing us out and emptying us, if he is finally to penetrate into us. . . . The function of death is to provide the necessary entrance into our inmost selves. It will make us undergo the required dissociation. It will put us into the state organically needed if the divine fire is to descend upon us.[1]

Thus Teilhard on the transforming power of death. In O'Connor we see it again in "The Displaced Person," where the hired man's wife, Mrs. Shortley, dies of a sudden convulsive seizure, trying desperately to clutch to her everything within her reach, including "her own moon-like knee." Suddenly, with a look of astonishment on her face, she collapses, "displaced . . . from all that belonged to her" and seeming to contemplate for the first time "the frontiers of her true country." But here the *seems* is in the story itself: "She *seemed* to contemplate . . . ," O'Connor writes. In fact, "Greenleaf" is hypothesis too: Mrs. May, dying, is described as *having the look*

---

1. Pierre Teilhard de Chardin, *The Divine Milieu* (New York, 1960) [Bernard Wall, General Editor of the English edition of Works of Teilhard de Chardin], 88–89. Sister Kathleen Feeley, S.S.N.D., discusses O'Connor's notations in O'Connor's own copy of *The Divine Milieu* and the Teilhard influence in general in her *Flannery O'Connor: Voice of the Peacock* (New Brunswick, 1972).

*of* "a person whose sight has been restored." Hypothesis, yes—but hypothesis that the reader is strongly urged to accept.

But we have said that the O'Connor doctrine was, even in comparison with that of other Catholics, eccentric, that it could even be repugnant; and perhaps there is nothing in the idea of the redemptive power of death, of death as rebirth, to bear this out. But having broached the work of Teilhard, we need only look at certain radical differences between his thought and O'Connor's to see how forbidding O'Connor is, even in the context of modern Catholic theology. She differs, that is, from Teilhard in one quite crucial area: in her attitude toward human life on earth, on the value and significance of worldly endeavor and experience.

It is almost enough, to indicate the distance between them, to quote Teilhard's inscription for *The Divine Milieu: Sic Deus Dilexit Mundum—for those who love the world.* Had Miss O'Connor ever used such a line, we can assume she would have used it mockingly and contemptuously, with the caustic irony of such titles as "A Good Man Is Hard to Find," "The Comforts of Home," "The Life You Save May Be Your Own," and "Good Country People." Clearly, for O'Connor, or at least for the implied author of the O'Connor tales (it will occasionally be useful to make this distinction), those who love the world—one is tempted to say not too much, but at all —are always to be held in contempt.

What Teilhard, on the other hand, wants to impress most deeply on his reader—and in fact he takes half of *The Divine Milieu* to do so—is that one need not, in fact must not, renounce the world to find God. For God is in and of the world, and all human endeavor—the extending, for instance, of the frontiers of human knowledge —is sanctified and justified and fully intended by the divine purpose for the universe. *The Divine Milieu* is addressed especially to those "waverers" who have come to feel that their instinctive love for life as they know it on earth separates them irrevocably from true Christianity. The great charge against Christianity in our time, he writes, is that it makes its followers inhuman. He describes the argument of the unbeliever as follows: " 'When a Catholic works with us, we invariably get the impression that he is doing so in a spirit of condescension. He appears to be interested, but in fact, because of his religion, he simply does not believe in the human effort as such. His heart is not really with us. Christianity nourishes deserters and false friends; that is what we cannot forgive.' " [2] And Teilhard grants that this objection, if it were true, "would be deadly." He himself often gives lyrical, almost Whitmanesque, expression to his adoration of the created universe; and of course he was by scholarly profession a geologist, occupied with the physical history of the earth, with mere matter. He believed that one ought wholeheartedly to participate in the life of this "holy place," the earth; to do so is to prepare oneself for life in Christ, for though in the end one surrenders self, one must have, after all, a self to surrender.

Life on earth, therefore, should not be "sad and ugly," Teilhard contends: "What would our spirits be, O God, if they did not have the bread of earthly things to nourish them, the wine of created beauties to intoxicate them, and the conflicts of human life to fortify them? What feeble powers and bloodless hearts your creatures would bring you if they were to succeed in cutting themselves off prematurely from the *providential* setting in which you have placed them!" [3]

How contrary all of this is to the doctrine of the O'Connor fiction. For what is oppressive about the O'Connor work as a whole, what is sometimes intolerable, is her stubborn refusal to see any good, any beauty or dignity or meaning, in ordinary human life on earth. A good

2. Teilhard, *The Divine Milieu*, 68.
3. *Ibid.*, 106.

indication of what must be called O'Connor's contempt for ordinary human life is the loathing with which she apparently contemplated the human body. She liked to describe faces—she hardly ever passed up an opportunity —and nearly all her faces are ugly. In the first novel, *Wise Blood,* this seems to be true without exception; human faces remind her of rodents, cats, hogs, mandrills, and vegetables; they are frog-like, hawk-like, gap-toothed, mildewed, shale-textured, red-skinned, stupid, demented, and simply "evil." Each part of the physiognomy comes in for its share of abuse; hair is likened to dirty mops and rings of sausages—it is said to stream down the face like ham gravy. One could continue the catalog—but the point, I think, is clear. Human beings are ugly in every way; the human form itself is distinctly unpleasant to behold; human life is a sordid, almost unrelievedly hideous affair. The only human act that is worthy of respect is the act of renouncing all worldly involvement, pleasure, and achievement.

Now, about the short stories, it is quite true that if we take the O'Connor stories individually they seem in this respect much less oppressive; but reading them back to back by volume—one of the ways, surely, that we expect to be able to read short stories—one may find his resistance mounting to the view of life that together they present. We may well grant that here is Mrs. May, comically self-adoring and self-righteous in spite of the fact that, as all can plainly see, she is a narrow-minded, deluded, ridiculous old fool; here is Asbury, a failed artist —contemptibly convinced of his total superiority over everyone else and yet childishly blaming his failures on his mother; here are poor old Mrs. Cope, Mrs. Turpin (who thanks God for good disposition), the appalling Ruby Hill. The images of these people rise up so graphically before us as we read—their manners, their speech are so cunningly done—that we freely respond to their reality within the story. Yet at the same time, one is dimly aware that the author is trying to make their stories say something, prove something about life, to which one cannot respond. For the revelation that O'Connor wanted to push us to—the truth about life that she wanted to force us to grant—was that these people represent, even at their comic worst, the norm of modern society. And one's own experience simply will not support such a view. With all one's admiration for the high technical brilliance of O'Connor's work, for her cunning selection of detail and delicate sense for nuance in speech and manners, and for the wonderfully controlled momentum with which her stories move—even with all this, one's pleasure is at least diminished by the fact that what the stories are moving *to* is a truth or hypothesis about life that sometimes seems hardly worth our consideration. We may feel that the stories would appear, seen from a certain point of view, nearly perfectly executed, but that that point of view is not ours, that—to restate the dilemma in Boothian terms—we cannot be the readers the stories require us to be.

The problem of assent to O'Connor's view of life, which it is possible to see as central to study of her work, is not one that has figured significantly in O'Connor criticism. Robert Drake, in a very sensible short study of O'Connor published in 1966, is one of the few writers who takes the doctrinal problem into account:

> What then about those readers who do not—or cannot— share Miss O'Connor's "Christian concerns"? How far can they enter into both the substance and the shadow of her work? There *does* seem a point beyond which such readers, even with the best will in the world, finally cannot go: they cannot honestly share the theological assumptions which *are* part of her donnée. Some tension in that quarter does seem inevitable, and perhaps finally does deny her the complete acceptance of some very discriminating readers.[4]

4. Robert Drake, *Flannery O'Connor* (Grand Rapids, Mich., 1966), a monograph published in the series "Contemporary Writers in Christian Perspective," 43.

This is a mild enough statement, certainly, but it makes
at least a tentative approach to an issue few have chosen
to confront.

Among the early O'Connor commentaries which touch
on this question, those of Granville Hicks are particularly
interesting. Hicks admired O'Connor; he was one of the
first important critics to pay attention to her work, and
he visited her several times at her farm in Milledgeville
and reported on these visits in the *Saturday Review*. But
it would seem that his feeling about her work continued
to be rather oddly mixed. Her apparent lack of feeling
for her ruined heroes, for instance, bothered and puzzled
him. "I was devastated," he wrote, "by the fate of the
reformer in 'The Lame Shall Enter First,' but Miss
O'Connor appears to believe that he got what he de-
served." [5] Among other critics southern writers have
been more willing than most to meet O'Connor on ideological ground—they have not evaded the fact that she
had a distinct and peculiar vision of life and that she
wanted, as she put it, "to get this vision across" to her
readers. Andrew Lytle, for instance, didn't mince his
words when he said of her stories that "no sermon could
be more terrifying."

The fact that we are not an age that in principle ap-
proves of didactic literature has been a complication in
O'Connor study. What we won't stand for, or say we
won't, is a work that "preaches"; and when we find in a
writer we otherwise admire incessant and not very subtle espousal of a special doctrine—and a narrow one at
that—we have our ways of evading it. Critics have been
fond of indirectly reminding readers that they must not
be prejudiced against O'Connor because she is a Catholic;
they say, in effect: "It's her art that matters, not what she
believed." But of course what she believed—the view of
the world that her stories offer us—does matter very

5. Granville Hicks, "A Cold, Hard Look at Humankind," *Saturday Review*, XLVIII (May 29, 1965), 23–24.

much. It seems strange indeed that face to face with the most fiercely religious literature of our time, we have had to take the evasive position that, as more than one critic has put it, "one need not after all give to these stories a religious interpretation." In the past few years, however, this situation has altered considerably, with the full gearing up—if one may put it that way—of the O'Connor critical industry since her death. Indeed a great many explanations of her religious thought and tracings of her religious themes and imagery through specific pieces have appeared; but the emphasis has been—particularly in academic criticism, which is generally more technical and less evaluative—much more on simple explanation than on assessment of the artistic problems that arise from O'Connor's peculiar doctrine.

T. S. Eliot was one of the writers who struggled with "the problem," as he termed it, "of poetic assent." Early in his career he believed that one should try to leave out of literary judgments one's personal beliefs; later he came to feel that such a thing was quite unnatural and impossible. At one point, he wanted to determine his own reasons for having come to think of Dante as a greater poet than Shakespeare, while at the same time not being able to prefer, in sheer literary genius, one to the other. Dante, he concluded, was for him the greater poet because Dante's Christian view of life was for him the truer vision. In considering his emotional response to the line of Dante's *In sua voluntade è nostra pace*, he came to believe that his response was at least heightened by the fact that he could believe this poetic statement to be literally true and by the fact that his own experience had "deepened its meaning." He wrote, "I can only conclude that I cannot in practice wholly separate my poetic appreciation from my personal beliefs." [6]

And how much more futile to try to make this separa-

6. T. S. Eliot, *Selected Essays* (New York, 1950), "Dante," 231.

tion in the reading of novels. One must, of course, be "objective" in the sense that one must not prejudge a writer's work on the grounds of his known ideology and that one must be willing to try to entertain, at least as a possibility, the view of the world his work supposes. Obviously there are more ways than one of looking at the world, of reading human experience; nevertheless, some ways are more interesting, revealing, impressive, and convincing than others, and some ways are not convincing at all.

Of course one does not wish to say, flatly, that the O'Connor view is "not convincing." Her reading, for instance, of the delusions, the weaknesses, the hypocrisy —in short, the bad—in human nature is, in itself, highly persuasive. But what is false in her work springs from her failure to see that though man is all the things herein implied, he is not only these things—and the total picture of human society that emerges from her work as a whole is one that is difficult to accept.

But the argument I have been making about the O'Connor work had better be bent now in another direction. Thus far I have deliberately left out of account, as much as possible, the celebrated O'Connor comedy. I have said that we have our ways, in American criticism today, of evading doctrinal problems in the writers we admire, and it seems that one of our ways of averting the religious fundamentalism in O'Connor has been to overemphasize her comedy. The reader who sums O'Connor up as "a fine comic writer"—*a comic writer,* that is, and just that —cannot finally be taken very seriously. One hears and reads this view of her rather skillfully put forth, but clearly it is not satisfactory. One may even grant that O'Connor's real forte was for comic writing, or that what one most enjoys in her stories is their comedy—but that does not make her "a comic writer." There is certainly very fine comic writing in the two novels, yet they are not *comic novels* in any accepted sense of the term. One need only read the final scenes of the two books to be sure of that. When, at the end of *The Violent Bear It Away,* we read of Tarwater moving ghost-like over the now sacred ground of Powderhead, feeling his hunger for the kingdom of God no longer as a pain but as a tide "rising in himself through time and darkness, rising through the centuries . . . building from the blood of Abel to his own," we would clearly be quite wrong to assume here the least touch of irony. And consider the final sentence of the book: "His singed eyes, black in their deep sockets, seemed already to envision the fate that awaited him but he moved steadily on, his face set toward the dark city, where the children of God lay sleeping." This is hardly comic writing. Yet one seems to encounter a great many O'Connor enthusiasts who confidently assure us that the fatal mistake is to "take her too seriously."

As for the comedy of the short stories, there are indeed a few stories that can safely be termed comedies and it is true that they are among her very best. Probably the three finest of this type are "The Life You Save May Be Your Own," "Good Country People," and "Parker's Back," a wonderfully funny story written during the last painful months of Miss O'Connor's life. One does not mean to say that these stories constitute a special set, clearly different from the other work—like all O'Connor works they are concerned with the problem of Christian belief; but the comically absurd aspects of the search for belief, which in O'Connor are seldom lost sight of completely, are continually in the foreground; the comic tone prevails, and the stories end, not—like most of the others —in sudden violent death or devastation for the protagonist, but as comic stories rightly do: in a much less painful ironic comeuppance. Hulga, for instance, in "Good Country People," has her wooden leg stolen by the phony Bible salesman she has been intending tenderly to convert to atheism. All three of these tautly controlled stories are full of exuberant comedy (one hardly knows anything funnier than the first meeting of Mr. Shiftlet and the old woman in the opening scene of "The Life You Save May Be Your Own"), and they are all "stretchers," parable-like tall tales in the tradition of frontier and southern country humor of which Faulkner's "Was" is perhaps the modern classic.

In most of the other short stories the comedy is much more caustic and more tense, and something sinister is at work all along, preparing the reader to have the grin wiped off his face at the end. Having quoted the final scene of "Greenleaf," we can use it again here as an example. This story contains one of the funniest O'Connor episodes: the fastidious Mrs. May discovering, on her walk through her precious woods, her farmhand's wife on her knees moaning over some newspaper clippings in some kind of primitive religious rite; but the story ends, as we have seen, with Mrs. May being gored to death by a bull—one of his horns piercing her heart, making the tree line look like a "dark wound in a world that was nothing but sky." Certainly the emotions elicited here are those of horror, surprise, and pain; we may feel that in a sense what happened to the prideful Mrs. May "served her right," but surely the dominant feeling here is not a satisfied sense of comic comeuppance. "Everything That Rises Must Converge" offers a similar example. What the reader most enjoys probably, throughout most of the story, is the comedy of manners of Julian and his mother —the son's glum, ill-natured intolerance, for instance, of his mother's fantasy-filled, childlike optimism. The episodes of the identical hats—the whole bus ride, in fact— is very shrewd comedy indeed; and when, getting off the bus, the mother offers her penny to the "little colored boy" and is walloped over the head by his fierce mama, her fantasy world finally collapses, her sense of what the world ought to be like—*was* like, in fact, she believes, in sweet southern times gone by—is dealt so deadly a blow that she falls to the sidewalk and dies:

He turned her over. Her face was fiercely distorted. One eye, large and staring, moved slightly to the left as if it had become unmoored. The other remained fixed on him, raked his face again, found nothing and closed.

"Wait here, wait here!" he cried and jumped up and began to run for help toward a cluster of lights he saw in the distance ahead of him. "Help, help!" he shouted, but his voice was thin, scarcely a thread of sound. The lights drifted farther away the faster he ran and his feet moved numbly as if they carried him nowhere. The tide of darkness seemed to sweep him back to her, postponing from moment to moment his entry into the world of guilt and sorrow.

Again, the grin wiped off our faces, we are sharply brought up—the real, the serious world lies suddenly before us. What seemed like play, what, seen in a certain light, seemed comical, is not so comical after all.

One raises this issue of the pervasiveness of the comedy in O'Connor not at all to prepare the reader for a tired struggle with this generic term, but because the tonal dimension in O'Connor is an important critical issue and because it is directly related to the central fact about this writer with which we have been dealing—the fact that she is a highly doctrinal writer whose view of human life often seems to modern readers strange and eccentric in the extreme. Such terms as comedy, farce, tragedy are, of course, loaded words in more ways than one. Those who see O'Connor as "a comic writer" can certainly find plenty of O'Connor's own statements to quote to their advantage. There is her famous statement about *Wise Blood,* that it was to her a "comic novel" but—and surely this is to beg the question—"like all comic novels" about "matters of life and death." There is an even stranger statement which describes as "comic" the bizarre and, surely for most readers, ultimately painful story "A Good Man Is Hard to Find." It is this latter story that I wish to pause here to examine in detail.

"A Good Man Is Hard to Find" is a story that contains some of the best O'Connor comedy but which ends in a

highly unsatisfactory way; and the failure of the final
scene—and hence of the story—seems to result from the
fact that a tonal shift that occurs midway through the
story finally runs out of control. The story is interesting
for our purposes in that we get a clearer view here than
anywhere else of the tonal problem that exists in one
degree or another in nearly all of O'Connor's fiction—the
problem, that is, of how to "take," how to react to, the
disasters that befall her characters.

This tale tells the story of a Georgia family (parents,
grandmother, and three children) who start out on a
vacation to Florida and are murdered along a roadside
by a trio of escaped convicts. Even one who had not read
the story might find it slightly odd that the writer of such
a tale would refer to it as O'Connor did (in an interview
at the College of St. Teresa) as "in a way a comic, stylized
thing" and therefore—and the logic here is perhaps particularly interesting—"not brutal." [7] How indeed would
one normally go about making a comedy of, for instance,
the killing of a baby? (One may also ask himself how
intrigued he would be likely to be with the comic pos-
sibilities of the massacre of *In Cold Blood*.)

But the point is: what kind of tonal oddity do we have
here and what is the nature of the problem that arises at
the end of the story?

## 2

"A Good Man Is Hard to Find" divides, in terms of
the time it encompasses, into two parts. The opening
page of the story describes the grandmother's attempt to
get the family to go to Tennessee instead of Florida on
their vacation; this serves as a kind of brief prologue to

7. O'Connor lectured at this college in Winona, Minnesota, in
October of 1960 and was interviewed by three students; the interview was later printed in a publication of the college, *Censer* (Fall,
1960).

the rest of the tale, all of which takes place the following
day as the family begins its fatal trip to Florida. The
trip itself then divides into two parts of its own. The
first part—the morning ride through middle Georgia with
the grandmother and children reacting to the sights along
the roadside and the grandmother entertaining the children with stories of her girlhood—is climaxed by a highly
entertaining scene at Red Sam's Barbecue. The second
part of the story may be said to begin, as the family starts
out again after lunch, with the grandmother's suggestion,
clamorously taken up by the children, that they turn off
the highway onto a certain dirt road which leads to an
old plantation house the grandmother had visited in her
youth. Or—even better—let us say that this scene in
which the aggravated father finally agrees to take the
turn onto the dirt road to the old house, serves as a transi-
tion between the two parts. For just off the dirt road, the
grandmother's cat, secretly smuggled into the car in a
basket, leaps onto Bailey's back and makes him wreck
the car. The car overturns into a deep ditch alongside
the road, and as the occupants are pulling themselves
together, the "hearse-like" car of the Misfit appears on
the road overhead. The major break in the story comes
with the following passage: "The road was about ten feet
above and they could see only the tops of the trees on the
other side of it. Behind the ditch they were sitting in
there were more woods, tall and dark and deep. In a few
minutes they saw a car some distance away on top of a
hill, coming slowly as if the occupants were watching
them." Our easy enjoyment of the domestic comedy of
this very ordinary family excursion begins at this point
sharply to subside. Here the story clearly takes a much
more solemn turn than we had expected it to—just *how*
solemn we are not yet sure. The Misfit and his two mates
now appear on the scene with drawn guns; they are as
sinister a trio as they could well be, and the main concern,

surely, of any reader from this point on is with what is going to happen to the family in the hands of the convicts.

The final scene will need to be studied in detail, but one may stop at this point to ask: what kind of story do we have up until the major tonal shift which occurs with the words *tall and dark and deep* in the above passage? Plainly it is a comic view of the family that we get in the first half of the story—and it is rich comedy indeed. The comedy issues, as it often does in O'Connor, from the author's dry, deadpan, seemingly unamused reporting of the characters' hilarious actions and appearance. Like many good modern comedies, the story is, in other words, all the funnier for not appearing to be told in a funny way. The grandmother, of course, is the largest and funniest figure, and she is the character from whose point of view the tale unfolds.

Like so many O'Connor vignettes, the opening scene is remarkable for what it accomplishes in a brief space; the vivid visual picture is etched in with swift, deft strokes, and the speech of the grandmother and the children (in this tableau-like scene the parents are silent) is also deftly, wittily done, so that even at the end of the first page we have a sharp sense of the personalities involved and a feeling for the kind of family life that is in question.

What is particularly impressive here is the way the visual image—the image of the family gathered in the living area of the house on what is perhaps a Sunday afternoon—takes shape from the ever-widening lens of the eye of the story. The opening sentence presents no image but tells of the grandmother's desire to go to Tennessee: "The grandmother didn't want to go to Florida. She wanted to visit some of her connections in east Tennessee and she was seizing at every chance to change Bailey's mind." Then we see, not the grandmother, but Bailey, sitting at the table over the *Journal*; and in the next sentence the grandmother herself comes into view behind the son, rattling at his head a piece of newspaper: "Here this fellow that calls himself The Misfit is aloose from the Federal Pen and headed toward Florida and you read here what it says he did to these people. Just you read it. I wouldn't take my children in any direction with a criminal like that aloose in it. I couldn't answer to my conscience if I did."

The grandmother gets no response from her shut-mouthed son, and as she wheels around to face the mother, the eye of the story widens again so that the mother, her face "as broad and innocent as a cabbage," is allowed to come into view sitting on the sofa silently feeding the baby his apricots. "You ought to take them somewhere else for a change so they would see different parts of the world and be broad. They never have been to east Tennessee," urges the grandmother. But the voice that replies comes from John Wesley, "a stocky child with glasses," and the eye of the story moves back again to bring into view the two older children reading the funny-papers on the floor.

"If you don't want to go to Florida, why dontcha stay at home?" . . .

"She wouldn't stay at home to be queen for a day," June Star said without raising her yellow head.

"Yes and what would you do if this fellow, The Misfit, caught you?" the grandmother asked.

"I'd smack his face," John Wesley said.

"She wouldn't stay at home for a million bucks," June Star said. "Afraid she'd miss something. She has to go everywhere we go."

"All right, Miss," the grandmother said. "Just remember that the next time you want me to curl your hair."

June Star said her hair was naturally curly.

The next morning the grandmother was the first one to the car, ready to go.

During the trip the next day we continue to relish the comical side of the grandmother's character: her busy-body backseat driving—which so infuriates her ill-natured son Bailey ("He didn't have a naturally sunny disposition like she did.") ; her awful humor (" 'Where's the plantation?' John Wesley asked. 'Gone with the Wind,' said the grandmother.") ; the inevitable childlike recounting of her early courting days ("She would have done well to marry Mr. Teagarden because he was a gentleman and had bought Coca-Cola stock when it first came out.").

The grandmother's costume for the trip is carefully etched in, detail by tiny detail:

> The old lady settled herself comfortably, removing her white cotton gloves and putting them up with her purse on the shelf in front of the back window. The children's mother still had on slacks and still had her head tied up in a green kerchief, but the grandmother had on a navy blue straw sailor hat with a bunch of white violets on the brim and a navy blue dress with a small white dot in the print. Her collar and cuffs were white organdy trimmed with lace and at her neckline she had pinned a purple spray of cloth violets containing a sachet. In case of an accident, anyone seeing her dead on the highway would know at once that she was a lady.

Now this business of being a lady, of doing *right* ("In my time . . . children were more respectful. . . . People did right then."), of being nice, begins rather early in the story to suggest the superficiality of the old lady's sense of good and evil, of what is right and good in the world. It is the grandmother who, when Red Sam of the barbecue palace says to her, "These days you don't know who to trust," delivers the crowning turn on the title line, "A good man is hard to find":

> People are certainly not nice like they used to be.

When Red Sam complains of his own misplaced trust in his fellow man—why did I let them fellers charge the gas they bought?—the grandmother is ready: "Because you're a good man!"

This conversation with Red Sam and his wife—the latter is perhaps the choice comic figure of the story—

certainly prefigures the climactic dialogue, with its "good man" theme, between the grandmother and the Misfit at the end. In the final scene the utter absurd comedy of the grandmother's values is pointed up by her belief that "a good man" wouldn't shoot "a lady"! The grandmother's pathetic strategy, even early on in the fatal encounter with the Misfit, comes to no more than that. When the grandmother says, "You wouldn't shoot a lady, would you?" the Misfit replies, "I would hate to have to," and the old lady blunders on with her grotesque appeal to the escaped murderer's sense of "niceness": " 'Listen,' the grandmother almost screamed, 'I know you're a good man. You don't look a bit like you have common blood. I know you must come from nice people!' "

But for all the grandmother's innocence and absurdity, one's feelings about her are by no means totally negative. If she is not endowed with insight into the eternal scheme of things—well, what of that? It is certainly possible to feel affection for the grandmother—though one may not be sure, as he reads, whether against the grain of the story or not. And yet surely there are lines and passages where the story is designedly setting our sympathies astir. The grandmother has a liveliness, curiosity, and responsiveness that the others seem to lack. Her true delight in telling stories ("she rolled her eyes and waved her head and was very dramatic") and in watching June Star dance ("the grandmother's eyes were very bright . . . she swayed her head from side to side") does not cast her in an ugly light. And the tone of such a passage as this, for instance, where she plays with the baby, is hardly ambiguous: "The grandmother offered to hold the baby and the children's mother passed him over the front seat to her. She set him on her knee and bounced him and told him about the things they were passing. She rolled her eyes and screwed up her mouth and stuck her leathery thin face into his smooth bland one. Occasionally he gave her a faraway smile." It is the grandmother, moreover, who sees the beauties of the Georgia landscape—the "blue granite," for instance, "that in some places came up to both sides of the highway; the brilliant red clay banks slightly streaked with purple; and the various crops that made rows of green lace-work on the ground." About the sentence that follows, "The trees were full of silver-white sunlight and the meanest of them sparkled," one may well ask: who sees the trees in this way? This line, it may be recalled, is the one singled out by Robert Fitzgerald, in his preface to *Everything That Rises Must Converge,* as evidence of O'Connor's "sense of natural beauty and human beauty" (even the meanest of her characters, Fitzgerald argues, can be said "to sparkle" as well). But are we to take the line as an aside of the author, or is it, in fact, strongly implied that the grandmother herself sees the trees in this way?

However that may be, one thing, I think, is clear: all in all, the comedy of the grandmother's portrait is not wholly without warmth, is not totally abusive and satiric. Certainly one cannot view the grandmother as one whose malignity of soul is such that one can welcome—be amused by, or, let us say, accept in a comic spirit—her fatal comeuppance at the hands of the Misfit. There is not, in other words, such heavy stylization, such gross distortion, in the characterization of the old lady that one's distance from her is great enough to preclude any pain that her tortured death might bring. Indeed, there is everywhere in the first part of this story the most scrupulous comic realism. It is the averageness, the typicality of this old grandmother that is so nicely caught by the story.

The story's careful realism is nowhere better seen than in the lunch scene at Red Sam's barbecue palace. Red Sam's memorable helpmate, for instance, is closely drawn on the cheerless, complaining, vacant-eyed, fish-wife of the country Georgia road-stop. Bringing in the family's barbecue plates, this wife delivers herself of another variation of the good-man-is-hard-to-find motif:

> "It isn't a soul in this green world of God's that you can trust," she said. "And I don't count nobody out of that, not nobody," she repeated, looking at Red Sammy.
> "Did you read about that criminal, The Misfit, that's escaped?" asked the grandmother.
> "I wouldn't be none surprised to see him. If he hears it's two cents in the cash register, I wouldn't be atall surprised if he . . ."
> "That'll do," Red Sam said. "Go bring these people their Co'Colas. . . ."

Much of the charm of this comic characterization one may certainly lay to O'Connor's gift for folk speech. (Ben Jonson's injunction to a hypothetical character—"Language most shows the man—speak! that I may see thee!" —was one O'Connor would have fully appreciated.)

Just before the descent of this story into the much darker and grimmer world of Part Two, the domestic comedy peaks again in the scene in which the father is tormented into making the turn down the dirt road to the plantation. The ritualistic rhythm, for instance, of the following scene is altogether too familiar for there to be any question of the reader's not being drawn into the experience of the family:

> The children began to yell and scream that they wanted to see the house with the secret panel. John Wesley kicked the back of the front seat and June Star hung over her mother's shoulder and whined desperately into her ear that they never had any fun even on their vacation, that they could never do what THEY wanted to do. The baby began to scream and John Wesley kicked the back of the seat so hard that his father could feel the blows in his kidney.
> "All right!" he shouted and drew the car to a stop at the side of the road. "Will you all shut up? Will you all just shut up for one second? If you don't shut up, we won't go anywhere."
> "It would be very educational for them," the grandmother murmured.

"All right," Bailey said, "but get this: this is the only time we're going to stop for anything like this. This is the one and only time."

"The dirt road that you have to turn down is about a mile back," the grandmother directed. "I marked it when we passed."

"A dirt road," Bailey groaned.

What we have, in other words, up until the moment when the grandmother, startled by the sudden embarrassed realization that memory has played a foul trick on her and that the old plantation is not on this road at all and not even in this state, jolts the basket and frightens Pitty Sing into springing with a snarl onto Bailey's shoulder, causing him to overturn the car—what we have is a skillful and richly entertaining domestic comedy of a not very lighthearted if not totally abusive kind. And if we have happened to read the inscription on the fly-leaf of *A Good Man Is Hard to Find*, on the page in fact facing this title story, we have certainly forgotten it—so little apropos does it seem to this funny family tale:

> THE DRAGON IS BY THE SIDE OF THE ROAD, WATCHING THOSE WHO PASS. BEWARE LEST HE DEVOUR YOU. WE GO TO THE FATHER OF SOULS, BUT IT IS NECESSARY TO PASS BY THE DRAGON.
> —St. Cyril of Jerusalem

No trace of a devouring dragon here! And though this epigrammatic dragon ought, perhaps—critically speaking—to be dealt with (is it the Misfit himself who plays the part in this story of a dragon by the side of the road?), if it crosses our minds, as we read, to wonder at all where the story is heading (and because O'Connor always *seems* to have her tales so well in hand, usually it doesn't cross our minds), the actual appearance of a death-dealing Misfit does not seem a very likely possibility. Some final sumptuous comic irony—harmlessly or

indirectly involving, perhaps, the real or an imagined
Misfit—is probably what one half-consciously expects.

Then the story breaks in two. Behind the wrecked family, sitting paralyzed with fear and shock in the ditch,
the woods, which seen a few hours ago from the highway were full of silver-white sunlight, are now described
as "tall and dark and deep." After the arrival of the convicts, the line of woods behind them will be said in fact
to *gape* "like a wide open mouth"; and when the first
member of the family is taken off to the woods and shot,
the wind will seem to the grandmother "to move through
the tree tops like a long satisfied insuck of breath." A
very different story indeed!

With the accident, then, and the appearance of the
armed convicts, the reader is much taken aback. "Why
this is not at all the kind of story I thought it was going
to be," he may feel—somewhat pleasurably; and he is
much affected by the terrifying situation the family finds
itself in and is suddenly hypersensitively alert to the
slightest detail of the action which follows. Other stories
of sudden disaster, when all had seemed to be going normally and well, may occur to him: Richard Wright's
"Big Boy Leaves Home," for instance, a story similar to
"A Good Man Is Hard to Find" in the perfectly gratuitous
nature of the suddenly descending misfortune—that is,
the sudden appearance of the hysterical white woman at
the edge of the swimming hole where the naked black
boys are playing on a summer day.

In "A Good Man Is Hard to Find" it is true that in a
trivial sense everything that happens is the grandmother's
fault: it was she who urged the turn-off onto the dirt
road, she who stowed Pitty Sing away in the basket and
who startled him into making Bailey wreck the car, and
it is she who finally dooms them all by recognizing the
Misfit and saying so: "You're The Misfit!" she shrieks;
"I recognized you at once!"; and any sense the reader

might have had that the story could continue in the comic mode is shattered by the Misfit's reply: "Yes'm, but it would have been better for all of you, lady, if you hadn't of reckernized me."

It is within the consciousness of the grandmother that we continue to experience the action of the story, even though the suffering of the mother and father is perhaps even more affecting than hers for being witnessed from the outside. The mother is shown from time to time sitting in the ditch, her left arm dangling helplessly and holding with the other the baby (who—a horrifying and somehow totally characteristic O'Connor detail—has gone to sleep). When the Misfit politely asks her if she would like to "step off yonder" into the woods with the killers, she replies "faintly": "Yes, thank you." Let a reader who feels that one can take this story too seriously ponder that detail—and with it the image, early on, of the father walking to his death with his son, holding the boy's hand.

But in any case it is to the author's purpose that the parents can credibly be made to remain for the most part dumb with shock. The grandmother has consistently been shown as "a talker," as the killer Bobby Lee puts it, and the effect of the situation on her is to make her try to talk her way out of it. The Misfit is a talker too, and the grandmother's insistence that he is really "a good man" who comes from "nice people" incites him to a long, querulous, rambling, rather absentminded reflection on the course of his life—his upbringing, his real or alleged wrongdoing, and the vexed (to say the least) state of his soul. What is of course the chief horror of the whole massacre scene is the way in which his casual discussion of these matters is punctuated by his polite commands for the execution of the other members of the family. The grandmother grows dizzier and dizzier as the murders are carried out, and finally she seems, in a sequence that has been given as many as half a dozen conflicting interpretations, to take leave of her tortured senses altogether: "[The Misfit's]

voice seemed about to crack and the grandmother's head
cleared for an instant. She saw the man's face twisted
close to her own as if he were going to cry and she mur-
mured, 'Why, you're one of my babies. You're one of my
own children!' She reached out and touched him on the
shoulder. The Misfit sprang back as if a snake had bitten
him and shot her three times through the chest." The
Misfit begins to clean his glasses, and this is the way the
story ends:

> Hiram and Bobby Lee returned from the woods and stood
> over the ditch, looking down at the grandmother who half
> sat and half lay in a puddle of blood with her legs crossed
> under her like a child's and her face smiling up at the
> cloudless sky.
>
> Without his glasses, The Misfit's eyes were red-rimmed
> and pale and defenseless-looking. "Take her off and thow
> her where you thown the others," he said, picking up the
> cat that was rubbing itself against his leg.
>
> "She was a talker, wasn't she?" Bobby Lee said, sliding
> down the ditch with a yodel.
>
> "She would of been a good woman," The Misfit said,
> "if it had been somebody there to shoot her every minute of
> her life."
>
> "Some fun!" Bobby Lee said.
>
> "Shut up, Bobby Lee," The Misfit said. "It's no real
> pleasure in life."

Thus the mean tonal snarl the story has wound itself into.
What *is* the reader to think or feel about anything in the
massacre scene? There is pain and shock but much that
mocks that pain and shock—the heavy comedy, for instance, indeed one might say the almost burlesque treatment, of the three killers. There is the feeling that though
we cannot help but pity the tormented family, the story
continues to demand our contempt for them. One feels
that somehow the central experience of the story—in spite
of the affecting, the chilling details surrounding these
deaths, in spite even of the not altogether abusive treatment of the grandmother in Part One—will elude anyone
who gives way to these feelings of pain and pity. If the

writer's task is, as Conrad said, to make us "see," what is here to be seen? Surely not that life is wholly senseless and contemptible and that our fitting end is in senseless pain.

Looking at the narrative skeleton of the story again, having corrected our original notion of it after reading the final half, what now do we have? An ordinary and undistinguished family, a family even comical in its dullness, ill-naturedness, and triviality, sets out on a trip to Florida and on an ordinary summer day meets with a terrible fate. In what would the interest of such a story normally lie? Perhaps, one might think, in something that is revealed about the family in the way it meets its death, in some ironical or interesting truth about the nature of those people or those relationships—something we had been prepared unbeknownst to see, at the end plainly dramatized by their final common travail and death. But obviously, as regards the family as a whole, no such thing happens. The family is shown to be in death just as ordinary and ridiculous as before. With the possible exception of the grandmother, we know them no better; nothing about them of particular significance is brought forth.

The grandmother, being as we have seen the last to die, suffers the deaths of all her family while carrying on the intermittent conversation with the Misfit, and any reader will have some dim sense that it is through this encounter that the story is trying to transform and justify itself. One senses that this conversation—even though our attention is in reality fastened upon the horrible acts that are taking place in the background (and apparently against the thrust of the story)—is meant to be the real center of the story and the part in which the "point," as it were, of the whole tale lies.

But what is the burden of that queer conversation between the Misfit and the grandmother; what power does it have, even when we retrospectively sift and weigh it line by line, to transform our attitude towards the seemingly gratuitous—in terms of the art of the tale—horror of the massacre? The uninitiated reader will not, most likely, be able to unravel the strange complaint of the killer without some difficulty, but when we see the convict's peculiar dilemma in the context of O'Connor's whole work and what is known of her religious thought, it is not difficult to explain.

The Misfit's most intriguing statement—the line that seemingly the reader must ponder, set as it is as the final pronouncement on the grandmother after her death—is from the final passage quoted above: "She would of been a good woman if it had been somebody there to shoot her every minute of her life." Certainly we know from the first half of the story that the grandmother has seen herself as a good woman—and a good woman in a day when good men and women are hard to find, when people are disrespectful and dishonest, when they are not nice like they used to be. The grandmother is not common but a lady; and at the end of the story we know that she will be found dead just as we know she wanted to be—in the costume of a lady. She was not common, and the Misfit, with his "scholarly spectacles," his courtly apology for not wearing a shirt, his yes ma'ams and no ma'ams, was not common either—she had believed, wanted to believe, or pretended to believe. "Why I can see you come from good people," she said, "not common at all." Yet the Misfit says of her that she *would* have been a good woman if somebody had been there to shoot her all her life. And if we take the Misfit's statement as the right one about the grandmother, how was she a good woman in her death?

A good woman, perhaps we are given to believe, is one who understands the worthlessness and emptiness of being or not being a "lady," of having or not having Coca-Cola stock, of "being broad" and seeing the world, of good manners and genteel attire. "Woe to them," said Isaiah, "that are wise in their own eyes, and prudent in their own sight." The futility of all the grandmother's values, the story strives to encapsulate in this image of her disarray after the car has overturned and she has recognized the Misfit: "The grandmother reached up to adjust her hat brim as if she were going to the woods with him but it came off in her hand. She stood staring at it and after a second she let it fall on the ground."

The Misfit is a figure that seems, one must say to the story's credit, to have fascinated more readers than any other single O'Connor character, and it is by contrast with the tormented spiritual state of this seeming monster that the nature of the grandmother's futile values becomes evident. We learn that the center of the Misfit's thought has always been Jesus Christ, and what becomes clear as we study over the final scene is that the Misfit has, in the eyes of the author, the enormous distinction of having at least faced up to the problem of Christian belief. And everything he has done—everything he so monstrously does here—proceeds from his inability to accept Christ, to truly believe. This is the speech which opens the narrow and emotionally difficult route into the meaning of the story:

> "Jesus was the only One that ever raised the dead," The Misfit continued, "and He shouldn't have done it. He thown everything off balance. If He did what He said, then it's nothing for you to do but thow away everything and follow Him, and if He didn't, then it's nothing for you to do but enjoy the few minutes you got left the best way you can—by killing somebody or burning down his house or doing some other meanness to him. No pleasure but meanness," he said and his voice had become almost a snarl.

The Misfit has chosen, at least, whom he would serve—has followed the injunction of the prophet in I Kings 18:21: "And Elijah came unto all the people, and said, How long halt ye between two opinions? if the Lord be God, follow him: but if Baal, then follow him." The crucial modern text for the authorial view here, which belongs to a tradition in religio-literary thought sometimes referred to as the sanctification of the sinner, is T. S. Eliot's essay on Baudelaire, in which he states: "So far as we are human, what we do must be either evil or good; so far as we do evil or good, we are human; and it is better, in a paradoxical way, to do evil than to do nothing; at least, we exist. It is true that the glory of man is his capacity for salvation; it is also true to say that his glory is his capacity for damnation." [8]

Thus observe how, in the context of these statements, "A Good Man Is Hard to Find" begins to yield its meaning. What O'Connor has done is to take, in effect, Eliot's maxim—"It is better, in a paradoxical way, to do evil than to do nothing"—and to stretch our tolerance of this idea to its limits. The conclusion that one cannot avoid is that the story depends, for its final effect, on our being able to appreciate—even to be startled by, to be pleasurably struck with—the notion of the essential moral superiority of the Misfit over his victims, who have lived without choice or commitment of any kind, who have in effect not "lived" at all.

But again, in what sense is the grandmother a "good woman" in her death, as the Misfit claims? Here even exegesis falters. Because in her terror she calls on the name of Jesus, because she exhorts the Misfit to pray? Is she "good" because as the old lady sinks fainting into the ditch, after the Misfit's Jesus speech recorded above, she mumbles, "Maybe he didn't raise the dead"? Are we to see her as at last beginning to face the central question of human existence: did God send his son to save the world? Perhaps there is a clue in the dead grandmother's final image: she is said to half lie and half sit "in a puddle of blood with her legs crossed under her like a child's and her face smiling up at the cloudless sky." For Christ said, after all, that "whosoever shall not receive the kingdom of God as a little child shall in no wise enter herein."

8. Eliot, *Selected Essays*, "Baudelaire," 373.

To see that the Misfit is really the one courageous and admirable figure in the story; that the grandmother was perhaps—even as he said—a better woman in her death than she had ever been; to see that the pain of the other members of the family, that any godless pain or pleasure that human beings may experience is, beside the one great question of existence, *unimportant*—to see all these things is to enter fully into the experience of the story. Not to see them is to find oneself pitted not only against the forces that torture and destroy the wretched subjects of the story, but against the story itself and its attitude of indifference to and contempt for human pain.

Now as it happens, "A Good Man Is Hard to Find" was a favorite story of O'Connor's. It was the story she chose to read whenever she was asked to read from her work, and clearly it held a meaning for her that was particularly important. Whenever she read the story, she closed by reading a statement giving her own explanation of it. (One version of that statement can now be read in the collection of O'Connor's incidental prose edited by Robert and Sally Fitzgerald titled *Mystery and Manners*.) She had come to realize that it was a story that readers found difficult, and she said in her statement that she felt that the reason the story was misunderstood was that the present age "not only does not have a very sharp eye for the almost imperceptible intrusions of grace, it no longer has much feeling for the nature of the violences which precede and follow them." [9] The intrusion of grace in "A Good Man Is Hard to Find" comes, Miss O'Connor said, in that much-discussed passage in which the grandmother, her head suddenly clearing for a moment, murmurs to the Misfit, "Why, you're one of my babies. You're one of my own children!" and is shot just as she reaches out to touch him. The grandmother's gesture here is what, according

9. Flannery O'Connor, *Mystery and Manners*, selected and edited by Sally and Robert Fitzgerald (New York, 1969), 107–14. The statement reprinted here was delivered at Hollins College.

to O'Connor, makes the story work; it shows that the grandmother realizes that "she is responsible for the man before her and joined to him by ties of kinship which have their roots deep in the mystery she has been merely prattling about so far," and it affords the grandmother "a special kind of triumph . . . which we instinctively do not allow to someone altogether bad."

This explanation does solve, in a sense, one of the riddles of this odd story—although, of course, one must say that while it is interesting to know the intent of the author, speaking outside the story and after the fact, such knowledge does not change the fact that the intent of the narrator manifested strictly within the story is damagingly unclear on this important point. And what is even more important here is that O'Connor's statement about the story, taken as a whole, only further confirms the fact that the tonal problem in this tale is really a function of our difficulty with O'Connor's formidable doctrine. About the Misfit, O'Connor says that while he is not to be seen as the hero of the story, yet his capacity for grace is far greater than the grandmother's and that the author herself prefers to think "that the old lady's gesture, like the mustard-seed, will grow to be a great crow-filled tree in The Misfit's heart, and will be enough of a pain to him there to turn him into the prophet he was meant to become." The capacity for grace of the other members of the family is apparently zero, and hence—Christian grace in O'Connor, one cannot help noting, is rather an expensive process—it is proper that their deaths should have no spiritual context whatever. O'Connor goes on to say (and here I am quoting from a version of the statement read at the University of Georgia and included in the O'Connor papers recently given to the Georgia College library by the author's mother):

"A Good Man Is Hard to Find" has been written very baldly from the orthodox Christian view of the world. I think we seldom realize just how deliberately we have to change our

sights to read such a piece of fiction. It is a view of the
world which is offensive to modern thought and particularly
to modern feeling. It is a view of the world which sees the
life of the body as less important than the life of the soul,
and the happiness of the individual as secondary to his ob-
servance of truth and his practice of charity.[10]

This, in fact, is rather mildly put. A statement in the
former version makes the reader's harsh dilemma even
clearer: "in this story you should be on the lookout for
such things as the action of grace in the Grandmother's
soul, and not for the dead bodies."

### 3

There are a number of other passages in O'Connor's
critical essays which can be brought to bear on these
questions of tone and belief which we have been discussing. In an address, for instance, delivered at Wesleyan
College in Macon, Georgia, in 1960, an address which is
a crucial document for study of her work, O'Connor made
the following statement:

> In 19th century American writing there was a good deal
> of grotesque literature which came from the frontier and
> was supposed to be funny; but our present grotesque char-
> acters, comic though they may be, are at least not primarily
> so. They seem to carry an invisible burden; their fanaticism
> is a reproach, not merely an eccentricity. I believe that they
> come about from the prophetic vision peculiar to any novel-
> ist, but particularly and, in these times, deliberately peculiar
> to the novelist whose [Christian] concerns I have been de-
> scribing.[11]

10. These papers were still in the process of being organized by
the Georgia College library in Milledgeville in the summer of
1972; they include a file containing a number of slightly different
versions of the O'Connor statement on "A Good Man Is Hard to
Find."

11. Flannery O'Connor, "Some Aspects of the Grotesque in
Southern Literature," *Cluster Review* [Mercer University, Macon,
Georgia], VII (March, 1965), 22. Available now in the above cited
*Mystery and Manners,* ed. Sally and Robert Fitzgerald.

It seems sensible to think of O'Connor's work as being
"comic, yet not primarily so"—perhaps, one could say, not
"ultimately so." The strange demands that her work
makes on the mind and the emotions are certainly under-
scored by her expressed contempt (in this same essay)
for sentimental, for "compassionate" writing, her apparent attempt (happily not always successful) to banish
feeling itself:

> I believe that in this country, the general reader has man-
> aged to connect the grotesque with the sentimental, for
> whenever he speaks of it favorably, he seems to associate it
> with the writer's compassion.
>
> It's considered an absolute necessity these days for writ-
> ers to have compassion. Compassion is a word that sounds
> good in anybody's mouth and which no book jacket can do
> without. It is a quality which no one can put his finger on
> in any exact critical sense, so it is always safe for anybody
> to use. Usually I think what is meant by it is that the writer
> excuses all human weakness because human weakness is
> human. The kind of hazy compassion demanded of the writer
> now makes it difficult for him to be anti-anything. Cer-
> tainly when the grotesque is used in a legitimate way, the
> intellectual and moral judgments implicit in it will have the
> ascendency over feeling.

Here O'Connor is, if anything, all too plain. A reader
who goes to O'Connor's critical prose in search of the ever-
elusive bridge to her thought which will somehow human-
ize her writings will probably find her critical statements
little less disturbing than her work. Just as the last line
of the passage above would lead one to expect, it is often
strict and passionless moral judgment that (even in the
face of vivid human suffering and devastation) the O'Connor fiction demands—and often on terms that are very
difficult to accept. Wayne Booth made the sensible observation that there is occasionally a writer whose private
vision of things we respect less and less the better we
understand it;[12] one wonders whether some such pattern

12. Wayne C. Booth, *The Rhetoric of Fiction* (Chicago, 1961),
395.

as this will emerge—or is emerging—among readers of O'Connor.

Of course a further explanation for the reader's dilemma in the highly ideological and evangelical O'Connor stories is that the judgments we are constantly pushed to make are really against ourselves. In O'Connor, as in other highly doctrinal writers—Richard Wright, for instance, and Georges Bernanos—to shock, confuse, and frighten the reader seems to be part of the authorial strategy. No one, I think, can now doubt that Flannery O'Connor saw herself as a writer with a gift of prophecy. In one of the last speeches Miss O'Connor made before her death, she said: "The Lord doesn't speak to the novelist as He did to his servant Moses, mouth to mouth. He speaks to him as He did to those two complainers, Aaron and Aaron's sister Mary: through dreams and visions, in fits and starts, and by all the lesser ways of the imagination." [13] The Lord may not speak this way or that—but he speaks! Her work must certainly be seen as, whatever else it is, a message and a warning, in the same way that the work of Bunyan is—and of Bernanos, Wright, and Lawrence—and in the way that the work of, say, Joyce, Faulkner, Warren, and Hemingway, is not.

O'Connor was continually deploring, in her public statements, the absence of common assumptions between herself and her secular readers; one sees over and over again a writer brooding on the radical differences in the Catholic (or, let us say, the religious-intuitive) and the secular views of the world and on what these differences imply for her art. "The Catholic novelist believes," she said, "that you destroy your freedom by sin; the modern reader believes, I think, that you gain it that way." Rationalist readers, she insists, are the "hard of hearing" to whom the "good" novelist must shout; they are the "blind" for whom he must draw "large and startling figures." What

13. Flannery O'Connor, "The Role of the Catholic Novelist," *Greyfriar* [Siena College, Loudenville, New York], VII (1964), 10.

the Christian writer really needs in order to be the best
writer he can is "a large intelligent reading audience
which believes Christ is God"; he needs others only because "not enough Catholics read good fiction," and in any
case the real proof of the Catholic writer's value is "the
satisfied Catholic reader." The Catholic novelist, moreover, is interested in moral distinctions, and "for the
modern reader, moral distinctions are usually blurred in
hazes of compassion." Miss O'Connor was inclined to de-
fine "good fiction" as something that could only be written
by religious-minded individuals, perhaps only by south-
erners fully attuned to the religious mind of the Bible
Belt.[14]

As we shall see, most of the O'Connor short stories can
be viewed as admonitory parables. "There was once a
proud woman of great estate," some of them seem to go,
"and this woman believed that the name of her saviour
should only be said in church." The reader must learn to
see himself in the absurd and deluded O'Connor characters—in the family of "A Good Man Is Hard to Find,"
for instance, in Julian and Mrs. May. As the radio evan-
gelists continue to tell their "lest-nin' audiences" every
day: "You got to know you're lost before you can be saved
—you got to see your condition for what it is." And if a
writer must use harsh and violent means to wrench the
unbeliever from his sweet bed of illusions, then he must.

Be all this as it may, what has been particularly troublesome about much of the O'Connor criticism of the past
decade has been the assumption that merely by virtue of
their power to pain and shock and disturb, the O'Connor

14. The O'Connor statements in this paragraph are taken from
"The Novelist and Free Will," *Fresco* [University of Detroit publi-
cation], n.s., I (Winter, 1963), 100; an interview of Miss O'Connor
by Gerard E. Sherry published in *Critic*, XXI (June–July, 1963),
29–31; O'Connor's essay, "The Church and the Fiction Writer,"
*America*, XCVI (March 20, 1957), 735 (now available in *Mystery
and Manners*, ed. Sally and Robert Fitzgerald); and the previously
cited *Greyfriar* essay, p. 10.

stories are somehow good stories. But surely it takes only a moment's reflection to remind us that a story that appalls and shocks may or may not be a good story; the crudest, most fragmented accounts of human events—accounts that depict, for instance, however artlessly, terrifying scenes of pain and death—have the power to stun and frighten. The excesses of the modern film in this regard have taught many of us to regard the aesthetically meaningless use of pain and shock with particular disgust. One does not mean to say that O'Connor's depiction of human suffering is—in terms of the author's peculiar point of view—gratuitous; the reader's frustration comes from not being able to share, from being, indeed, sometimes repelled by, the authorial attitude towards the events described.

There is a sense in which, as I have suggested, the O'Connor stories are designed as calculated affronts to humanistic thought. One often has the feeling, in reading an O'Connor story, of being initially quite in harmony with the authorial viewpoint, of enjoying the story exactly in the way it seemed meant to be enjoyed, and then of being—often almost without warning—shaken violently off the track, so that one feels almost deliberately shut out from the final, and thus the overall, experience of the story. This state of affairs is disconcerting indeed; for one assumes that the power that the narrative artist has generally strived to acquire has been the power finally to accomplish the full seduction of the reader, to bring him finally into full and exciting union with the teller of the tale.

And yet of course, even with O'Connor, the aim really *was* to make the reader *see*, above all the futility of his life and the saving power of Christ; but many of us are simply too far gone in anthropocentric irreligiosity to make very good pupils for such a course of study. Much of the Christian art of the past still has, of course, the

power to make us feel, if not the truth, at least the beauty
and appeal of a certain side of Christian thought, of its
doctrine, for instance, of a loving savior in whom all one's
pain and failure can be laid; one thinks, for instance, of
the gentle Christian lyricism of the poet Hopkins, and of
the shattering drunken monologue of the wretched Mar-
meladov in *Crime and Punishment*. Christian art is not
dead for us, and there would still seem to be a great deal
of common ground between humanistic Christian thought
and secular humanism for the Christian artist to occupy
if he can. But perhaps the crucial word here is "humanistic." For certainly O'Connor's Christian faith was as
grim and literalistic, as joyless and loveless a faith, at
least as we confront it in her fiction, as we have ever seen
in American letters—even, perhaps, in American theology.

If, on the other hand, we look abroad, we find a number
of modern-day European Catholic and Anglo-Catholic
writers of a very similar religious and artistic persuasion:
in England there was T. S. Eliot (and O'Connor may also
have had a special and rather peculiar debt to Graham
Greene), and in France such writers as Bernanos and
Mauriac.[15] Like O'Connor, these men were Christian writers of a fiercely conservative, literalistic persuasion; and
it probably should not surprise us that in a day when true
Christian belief seems more and more anachronistic, the
voice of the beleaguered Christian artist should take on
a bitter and belligerent tone. That one among them should
have addressed to his readers, at an otherwise tender moment in his story, such words as these will show what I
mean :

15. There are a number of interesting analogues of O'Connor
works among the writings of Mauriac (*Thérèse Desqueroux*),
Greene (*Brighton Rock*), and Eliot (especially *The Family Re-
union*). See an article by the present writer titled "Flannery
O'Connor and the Sanctified Sinner Tradition," *Arizona Quarterly*,
XXIV (Autumn, 1968), 223–39.

You who know nothing of the world but the colors and
sounds which have no substance, you sentimental souls and
poetic mouths where the bitter truth would melt like a sugar-
plum—tiny souls, tiny mouths—this is not meant for you.
Your wickedness is in keeping with your delicate nerves and
sensitive brains, and the Satan of your peculiar ritual is
only your own defaced image, for the slave of the carnal
world is his own Satan. The monster looks down at you and
laughs, but he hasn't got you in his grip. He is not to be
found in your novels, you drivelers, not in your blasphemies
and idiotic spite. He is not in your avid eyes, in your
treacherous hands, in your ears that hear not. In vain you
will seek him in the most secret flesh which your pitiful lust
will pierce without ever finding peace, and the blood on the
lips that you bite is tasteless and pale.

This passage is from Bernanos' *The Star of Satan* and
occurs just before the author describes a young priest's
purification of heart as he prays in his church.[16] O'Connor never spoke, of course, such words as these—she never
spoke directly to the reader at all. But the rage and the
bitterness—the spite—was often there, just as in Bernanos.

And yet with all that one has now said about the philosophical and tonal dilemma in O'Connor, there is also a
great deal to say positively about her art, and it will take
the rest of this study to, in a sense, redress the balance.
One can be sure that O'Connor felt, along with the temp-
tation simply to punish and outrage her rationalist readers, a deep desire to communicate a vision of life the oddness of which no one was more aware of than she herself.
A strategy for finding some common ground between herself and her readers did certainly exist in her work and
was often highly successful.

But to begin at the beginning, we will look first at the
earliest and strangest O'Connor book, the novel *Wise
Blood*.

16. George Bernanos, *The Star of Satan*, trans. Pamela Morris
(Paris, 1926), 348.

## Chapter II

# *Wise Blood*

O'Connor's short stories are certainly better known to the wider reading public than her novels; and not only the general reader but also her critics, close literary friends, and fellow writers have thought of her primarily as a short story writer. It has been the stories that have won the prizes and acclaim, and it was the fourth book, the posthumous story collection *Everything That Rises Must Converge*, which seemed to settle her claim to literary eminence. Yet it is also true that with all their defects the two novels contain some of O'Connor's best writing. In these books there are passages of great charm and of a serene beauty of a different order from anything in the stories, passages which present a side of O'Connor's mind and art which needed the amplitude of the novel to be expressed and which would always have been constricted by the short story form. Two passages, in particular, may be cited: first, the last chapter of *Wise Blood,* which tells the penance and death of the half-crazy—by most people's lights—religious zealot Hazel Motes; and second, the first two chapters of *The Violent Bear It Away,* which tell, as a reflection of a twelve-year-old boy as he gets drunk on his great uncle's moonshine on the day of the uncle's death, the story of the boy's life with this fanatical old uncle in a backwoods clearing in Tennessee.

Now it is quite true that one cannot think of O'Connor as having mastered the novel form in the way that she

mastered the short story; it is clear that it was the shorter
form that came to her most naturally and that she had
much greater difficulty with the novel. The first novel,
*Wise Blood,* constitutes an almost classic set of unsolved
novelistic problems. She obviously found herself hard
pressed, for instance, to sustain the narrative line for two
hundred pages; though many of the episodes of the book
are artfully patterned in themselves, the overall structure
is somewhat crude. There is, for one thing, a strange, ag-
gravatingly labored sub-plot, the story of the moronic zoo-
keeper Enoch Emery, that will not sink into the stream
of the narrative as it should.

O'Connor seemed to need, in other words, a short form
that she could bring utterly under control; she did not
want something that was liable—as she herself might
have put it—to run away with her, to get her in too deep,
to get her in a fix that she couldn't get out of. An image
that comes to mind is of Hazel Motes, who as a boy was
afraid of following Jesus "out into the dark where he
might walk on the water and not know it and then know
it and drown." Even the abbreviated novel form that
O'Connor tried in *Wise Blood,* and later with more success in *The Violent Bear It Away,* was to give her considerable trouble. She would have despaired at the very idea
of attempting the complicated, sprawling, abundant novel
that her southern male compatriots were writing—Wolfe,
somewhat before her time of course, Faulkner, Styron,
and Warren. Nothing was more foreign to her than that;
and like many woman writers, her impulse, one feels,
when she confronted such works must have been to pitch
in and clean them out and straighten them up. Yet another
factor that helps explain, it would seem, her proclivity for
the short story was the fact of her illness and her almost
certain sense—for the same disease had killed her father
at forty-two—that she did not have time to waste on
something that might take a great deal of one's time and

then not work out. With a story, she once said, "you know you've got something sooner." [1]

But if in her art what O'Connor liked best was a small, nearly perfectible form, there was at variance with this need another need that may have gone even deeper: the desire to tell a certain rather grand story, one that would not fit into the small vessel of the short story. I am referring, of course, to the story of the Christian travail, of the quest for true belief and holiness, as opposed to the kind of tale she had to content herself with in the short stories—that is, satiric, contemptuous tales about the lives of the godless, tales that deal not with true religious experience, but with the emptiness and futility of the irreligious life. The desire that O'Connor felt to tell the full story of the Christian passion seems to have been something that ordinarily she did not allow to rule her, but the fact is that twice in the normal business of writing short stories, she was overtaken by it. And in fact we know that both novels grew out of pieces that were originally conceived as short stories.

Even within the short stories O'Connor sometimes managed a tenuous, skimpy tracing of the making of a Christian; the story studied in the preceding chapter, "A Good Man Is Hard to Find," represents one such attempt, and as unpromising as the Misfit might seem for the protagonist of a novel, both her novels are attempts to tell the full religious history of just such a man. In "A Good Man Is Hard to Find" we do not see the Misfit winning his battle against unbelief, but we know that he has taken the first, all-important step: he has begun, the implication is, very early in his child's life, the rabid, all-consuming search for religious truth that, if followed bravely and pridelessly enough, can eventually bring man—literally

1. C. Ross Mullins, "Flannery O'Connor, An Interview," *Jubilee*, XI (June, 1963), 32.

does bring the heroes of the two novels—to true belief and holiness.

Aside from "A Good Man Is Hard to Find," only two stories have the kind of obsessively religious characters that O'Connor wrote about in her novels: there is the young tramp, Johnson, of "The Lame Shall Enter First," a story that was a spin-off, one might say, of *The Violent Bear It Away*; and O. W. Parker of "Parker's Back," the man who has a face of Christ tattooed on his back to please his wife and who is finally himself trapped—looking at his back in double mirrors—in the fierce embrace of Christ's eyes. There are a few other stories that deal, as these two do, with real religious experience, but in a much milder, gentler way: "The Artificial Nigger," for instance, describes the terrifying and chastening experience of an old man and his grandson on a visit to the city; "The River" is an account of a pathetic search of a small boy for Christ in the river where he had been baptized and ends with the boy's drowning. All of these stories contain, that is, sympathetically drawn protagonists who suffer some kind of religious ordeal—and one may add to this group one more story, a very adroit tale that we will examine in detail in the last chapter, "A Temple of the Holy Ghost," which is about a young girl's attempt to penetrate the mystery of a hermaphrodite's contention that it is "a temple of the holy ghost."

But the heroes of the novels stand out, as I have said, with the Misfit and Johnson, as the most peculiar, most highly wrought and forbidding, of the O'Connor characters. One can hardly think, in fact, of another novelist who has undertaken to interest the reader in heroes so thoroughly divested of normal (or, as one must constantly repeat, what most of us take to be "normal") human attributes. These characters we rarely ever catch, for instance, in the simplest expressions of human kindness or love; their single obsession is with their search for religious truth, and the point is that to prosecute their

search, *they will go to any lengths.* Hazel Motes and Tarwater both commit murder, and they seem to do it—quite
unlike their quasi-progenitor Raskolnikov—without re-
morse.

It is not surprising that early reviewers of *Wise Blood,*
and even of *The Violent Bear It Away,* were as baffled as
they were by O'Connor's religious heroes; often they
seemed to be perplexed as to whether these wildly fanatical and violent characters could really be drawn as heroic
figures, as saved, superior individuals. Near the end of
*Wise Blood* Hazel's landlady is similarly amazed to discover that Hazel is punishing himself by wearing strands
of barbed wire around his chest (a Georgia redneck's version of the hair shirt). The landlady says it's not "natural," it's not "normal." "It's like one of them gory stories," she says, "it's something that people have quit doing
—like boiling in oil or being a saint or walling up cats."
She says, "There's no reason for it. People have quit doing it." And Hazel replies, "They ain't quit doing it as long
as I'm doing it."

Miss O'Connor might have said as much about her queer
brand of fiction. To this day many readers cannot accept,
even in the face of the boldest evidence, what is clearly
the authorial attitude towards O'Connor's religious heroes,[2] but any one who is still in doubt probably ought to

2. One of the more recent O'Connor studies to deny the religiosity of O'Connor's fiction is that of Josephine Hendin, *The
World of Flannery O'Connor* (Bloomington, 1970). Hendin's por-
trayal of O'Connor as a woman whose violent but deeply suppressed
rejection of the role she was expected to play in southern society
accounts for the belligerence—and what Hendin sees as the
"nihilism"—of her fiction is sometimes interesting; but one must
reject altogether this critic's view of O'Connor's thought and hence
her reading of the O'Connor works themselves. Hendin sees both
novels as negativistic "novels of initiation" in which neither hero
actually "grows up." She writes that Tarwater ends up badly as an
empty "replica of the prophet [old Tarwater] and Motes turns
into a logical absurdity: a suffering mechanical man." She says
both characters "suffer from ice in the blood, from a pervasive
emotional exhaustion broken only by episodic violence" and that

reread the last chapters of the two novels. The point, the message, of these books is as clear, once you begin to see it, as it could possibly be: it is not they—these religious heroes—who are sick, who are freaks, but we ourselves; it is we who cannot give up all—who cannot give up anything—for Christ, who are sick, who have been freaks so long we cannot see ourselves for what we are. In defense of her obsessed religious characters, O'Connor might have used a line from Eliot's *The Family Reunion*:

> The one taking the opposite direction
> Will appear to run away.

What these books tell us is that the struggle for acceptance of the will of God is the most terrifying struggle man can face. To achieve and then to sustain true belief and true surrender to Christ, to suppress the prideful self, is a never-ending torment. Bernanos said, in a passage that provides a key to the O'Connor novels: "The witness of saints must be torn with irons out of their bodies." [3] O'Connor certainly saw her religious heroes as men whose fundamental integrity, in spite of the desperate paths of violence into which their search sometimes betrays them, nevertheless shines brilliantly forth from the dull, doomed, meaningless lives of the uncommitted people around them. In *Crime and Punishment* the police chief Porfiry speaks, in one of those remarkable interviews with Raskolnikov, words that could be spoken almost without change—were there a Porfiry in *Wise Blood* to speak them—of Hazel Motes and his invention of the Church Without Christ:

> You invented a theory, and you were ashamed because it went wrong and because it turned out to be not even very original! It proved mean and base, it is true, but that does

---

they both end in an "essential emotional death that preserves them in their passive, lonely fury" (pp. 60–61).

3. These are words Bernanos attributes to the dying curé in *The Star of Satan*, 348.

not make you hopelessly mean and base. You are not mean
and base at all! At least, you did not deceive yourself for
long, but in one leap reached the farthest extremity. Do you
know how I regard you? As one of those who could allow
themselves to be disembowelled, and stand and face their
torturers with a smile—if they had found a faith, or found
God.[4]

## 2

As one looks over the early reviews of *Wise Blood*, it is
easy, with the advantage of twenty years' hindsight, to
cast at the reviewers quite well-aimed stones. Not more
than two or three had any clear understanding of what
the book is really about, of the fact that it is a bitterly
serious, if sometimes outlandishly comic, version of the
Christian travail. This misunderstanding we can now attribute partly to the sometimes weak signals of the novel
itself and partly to the fact that the book was so totally
unexpected that readers simply could not believe, were not
prepared by much of anything in American letters to believe, what was before their eyes. One novel of modern
times which one might have expected to have come to
mind is Nathaniel West's *Miss Lonelyhearts*; this book is
in many ways as eccentric a tonal hybrid as *Wise Blood*,
and it is a book under whose influence Miss O'Connor
probably came as she was writing her own first novel.[5]
No one seems, however, to have made the association; and
in any case, even *Miss Lonelyhearts* is in one important
respect a less forbidding book than *Wise Blood, i.e.,* in
that West's sense of life and of human suffering is not,
finally, for all his weirdly contorted way of expressing it,
nearly so peculiar as is O'Connor's.

Today we have come to understand *Wise Blood*; we
know that Hazel Motes is drawn as a sympathetic hero,

4. Feodor Dostoevsky, *Crime and Punishment,* trans. George
Gibian (New York, 1964), 440–41.
5. See Robert Fitzgerald's introduction to *Everything That Rises
Must Converge* (New York, 1965), xv.

that the novel makes very little sense read any other way. But what is interesting is that it is still possible to feel about the overall success of the book much as the early reviewers did. The general feeling was that in spite of certain odd strengths, the book did not, finally, much commend itself; its action was too bizarre, too unreal, to sustain the reader's interest. The reviewers complained that the characters were "a race of sports" in whose fates it was impossible to take any real interest, that the O'Connor world was simply "insane . . . peopled by monsters and submen," that the plot consisted chiefly of "the private twitchings of several almost totally dislocated individuals," that Hazel himself was "so repulsive that one could not become interested in him." [6] It is hard to believe that at least the broadest comic effects of the book could have been missed by these readers, but there was almost no expressed appreciation of the book's humor. Also, since few readers could see Hazel Motes as anything but a rather aimless assault on southern fundamentalist fanatics, the lyrical account of his final surrender and death apparently made little impression.

With all this, however, one quality of the book—its clear and vivid language—quite regularly won the admiration of these early readers, and it is a quality that continues to earn one's respect as one studies over the book today. R. W. B. Lewis, writing in the *Hudson Review,* spoke of O'Connor's prose as "remarkably pure and luminous";[7] the reader will see how right the sentences in *Wise Blood* could be as he reads or rereads the passages quoted below.

6. The reviews referred to are, in the order mentioned: William Goyen, "Unending Vengeance," *New York Times Book Review,* May 18, 1952, p. 4; Isaac Rosenfeld, "To Win by Default," *New Republic,* CXXVII (July 7, 1952), 19; R. W. B. Lewis, "Eccentrics' Pilgrimage," *Hudson Review,* VI (Spring, 1953), 144–50; and Oliver LaFarge, "Manic Gloom," *Saturday Review,* XXXV (May 24, 1952), 22.

7. See his review in *Hudson Review* as cited above.

Even in the book's language, of course, there are occasional extravagances which O'Connor was to deny herself in later works; one thinks, in particular, of the sometimes excessive figurative language used to describe the grotesque looks and gestures of the characters.

Looking at the book as a whole from our own perspective, it is certainly true that among O'Connor's four queer, decidedly eccentric books, *Wise Blood* is by far the queerest. It presents, for instance, the most remorselessly squalid picture of human life. In spite of a broad range of comic effects, including a few memorably hilarious moments and an occasional comic playfulness, the narrator's surface pretense at presenting her grim picture of human life in the name of simple comedy is very thin indeed. One does not know whether to attribute the difference in the degree of harshness between this and later books— they are harsh enough, after all—to a modulation in O'Connor's personal view of things after *Wise Blood* or to what may have been her deepening instinct for survival as an artist with something serious to say; it may be that changes in later works reflect simply an attempt to refine her method of trying to get the world to listen to a message it did not want to hear. O'Connor was to describe in *The Violent Bear It Away* a similar dilemma in the life of her old country prophet Tarwater. He had been using such explosive means of trying to bring his worldly-wicked sister to repentance that she had convinced people that he was dangerous and had to be put away: "His [young Tarwater's] uncle had been in the asylum four years because it had taken him four years to understand that the way for him to get out was to stop prophesying on the ward. . . . But at least in the asylum the old man had learned caution and when he got out, he put everything he had learned to the service of his cause. He proceeded about the Lord's business like an experienced crook." In a sense, O'Connor herself never stopped "prophesying on the ward," but her prophecy was to grow, like old Tarwater's, in caution and cunning over the years.

Her first book, for instance, is certainly the one with the most baldly intrusive narrator. And one is not referring merely to the fact that the author sometimes speaks to the reader rather directly—she never does so, in any case, on the substantive issues of the book—though it is clearly the case that the narrative mode here is much freer in every respect than it is later on; in *Wise Blood,* for instance, the point of view is allowed to float from character to character even within scenes. What is intrusive is simply the way in which the authorial presence is constantly felt through the weird, if ostensibly dramatic and objective, shaping of the wider world in which the main characters move. As the people in *Wise Blood* go about their business and pleasure in the town of Taulkinham—on the streets, in the roominghouses and filling stations, at the zoo, in the Frosty Bottle, the Paris Diner, and Slade's used-car lot—we note, perhaps with growing surprise and curiosity, that not only the main actors, but all the incidental people they encounter, are hideous and ridiculous; they are stupid, mean, and brutish. And it is not at all that the hero *sees* them as hideous and ridiculous —on the contrary, we seem to have it on the narrator's own authority.

The inner struggle of Hazel Motes is very similar to that of young Tarwater in *The Violent Bear It Away,* but Hazel's *bellum intestinum* does not so powerfully overwhelm the imagination as Tarwater's does. Doubtless this is true partly because Hazel's struggle is not held so steadily in view—in terms of the action of the book—as is Tarwater's in the later novel, but also because in *Wise Blood* there is another subject constantly vying with it for our attention. To this other subject we are so busy reacting with awe and astonishment that the war in Hazel's soul seems, throughout much of the book, almost inciden-

tal—a state of affairs which may explain the failure of
the early reviewers even to grasp the nature of Hazel's
predicament. This other subject is the curious sensibility,
not of the hero, but of the author. What fascinates the
reader in *Wise Blood,* even more than in other O'Connor
works, is the nature of the eccentric sensibility operating
behind and outside the novel, setting such a queer stage
for the hero to act out his misadventures on.

It is O'Connor's method here to light up every corner
of that queer stage, to dwell for at least a brief abusive
moment on all the faces we glimpse on the edges of the
main action, to report, with what seems to be unsurprised
contempt, all the exchanges the principal characters have
in carrying on their daily business. And the amazing ugliness and meanness of that passing parade is what shapes
our sense of what the world—not just this or that unhappy individual, but people in general—is like for the
author. One can turn to almost any page and find an example of what I mean. No one is likely to forget the policeman who (for no discernible reason except that people
are mean, this is the way they act) pushes Hazel's old
Essex off the cliff; or, a few pages later, the cops who find
the vagrant Hazel half-conscious in a ditch on a winter
night and casually beat him to death with their night-
sticks; or the remarkably gratuitous ferocity of the fake
gorilla whose hand Enoch Emery stands in line to shake
at the movie house. Enoch's father is the villain (though
what meaning can a concept like villainy have in such a
world?) of another typically grim *Wise Blood* anecdote:
"Enoch was usually thinking of something else at the moment Fate began drawing back her leg to kick him. When
he was four years old, his father had brought him home
a tin box from the penitentiary. It was orange and had
a picture of some peanut brittle on the outside of it and
green letters that said, A NUTTY SURPRISE! When Enoch
had opened it, a coiled piece of steel had sprung out at
him and broken off the ends of his two front teeth." If a

character buys a cup of coffee, he buys it from a mannish woman with a sour look and a "once-white uniform clotted with brown stains" who drinks whiskey all day from a jar under the counter—or from one with "a big yellow dental plate and the same color hair done up in a black hairnet." A woman seen at the zoo pool is said to have a "long and cadaverous" face, "with a bandage-like bathing cap coming down almost to her eyes, and sharp teeth protruding from her mouth." Our first glimpse of Hazel's landlady shows her to be a "tall, bony woman, resembling the mop that she carried upside down." And it is finally on the merciless marshalling of all these repugnant details, the puzzling zeal of the narrator to shut out from her human scene anything of good or beauty whatever, that our attention becomes strangely fixed.

The female lead in the story is a kind of ultimate grotesque named Sabbath Hawks, the child of the street preacher and phony blind man. One of Sabbath's more entertaining qualities is her repertoire of grisly stories about people she has known, such as the one about an old woman who breaks out in "welps" every time she meets up with anything good. Was O'Connor burlesquing herself —or her narrator, at least—with this story? It is amusing, in any case, to read it as commentary on the narrator's own aversion to "the least good thing":

> There was this child once . . . that nobody cared if it lived or died. Its kin sent it around from one to another of them and finally to its grandmother who was a very evil woman and she couldn't stand to have it around because the least good thing made her break out in these welps. She would get all itching and swoll. Even her eyes would itch her and swell up and there wasn't nothing she could do but run up and down the road, shaking her hands and cursing and it was twicet as bad when this child was there so she kept the child locked up in a chicken crate. It seen its granny in hell-fire, swoll and burning, and it told her everything it seen and she got so swoll until finally she went to the well and wrapped the well rope around her neck and let down the bucket and broke her neck.

Now however this may be, there is, of course, in *Wise Blood*, one individual meant to earn the reader's admiration. Moving through the sick, blasted, animalistic world of the novel is a hero whose virtue, however queerly manifested, is meant to blaze from this barren ground all the more wonderfully forth—one who finally succeeds in delivering himself from the tyranny of his own blood and finding his way "backwards," as O'Connor puts it, "to Bethlehem."

The title concept of the book is clearly an ironical one— one's blood is not "wise"; to believe that it is (that one can rely simply on self) is the classic fundamental error of prideful mankind. This concept is one of the central recurrent themes of the book, a bottom stone on which the author attempts to erect the meaning of the strange experience of the characters. As we shall see, it is this concept that seems to connect—less dramatically than one would wish—the stories of Hazel and his would-be friend Enoch Emery. Enoch is the one character consciously and literally obsessed, we are asked to believe, with the mysterious power of his blood—its power, that is, to control everything he does, even against his will. Throughout the Enoch sections of the book Enoch's blood is leading him on an absurd chase towards some secret goal known only to itself.

Early in the story Hazel, who had just gotten out of the army, where he has learned with relief that man has no soul and that there is no Jesus to dog one's steps, meets Enoch and the Hawkses at a sidewalk demonstration of potato peelers. Enoch begins right away his desperate attempts to befriend Hazel, but Hazel is never to treat him with anything but total contempt. Hazel is much more attracted to the street preacher and fake blind man Hawks; he wants to practice his blasphemies on this apparent believer. However, the phony Hawks, as well as nearly everybody else in the book, sees right away what the careful reader will gradually come to accept as the

truth about Hazel: that deep down, he is a Jesus-hog himself—a "Christian *malgré lui*," as O'Connor smartly
phrases it in her preface—and is out to find anything he
can that will break the back of his new-found nihilism.
Even Enoch sees what Hazel is really after. When Hazel
persists in following the Hawkses through the streets,
ostensibly to torment them with his blasphemies, Enoch
says, "I knew when I first seen you you didn't have nobody nor nothing but Jesus. I seen you and I knew it."
Hazel refuses to go off with Enoch for some nighttime
adventures in the city, whereupon Enoch snivels like a
baby and taunts him with the attention he himself has
gotten from Sabbath Hawks: " 'She tole me where they
lived and ast me to bring you—not you bring me, me bring
you—and it was you follering them.' His eyes glinted
through his tears and his face stretched in an evil crooked
grin. 'You act like you think you got wiser blood than
anybody else,' he said, 'but you aint! I'm the one has it.
Not you. *Me.*' " Thus is launched the wise blood theme of
the novel, and the question projected: who *does* have wise
blood—Hazel or Enoch?

The whole of a following chapter is given over to an
account of the daily rites Enoch's blood forces him through
after he gets off work at the zoo. Every day, we are told,
he goes first to the zoo's swimming pool and hides in the
abelia bushes to watch the women swim. Then he goes to
the Frosty Bottle for a chocolate milkshake, after that to
look at the animals—which he hates and in a sense envies
—and then to the zoo museum, the "secret center" of the
park, to look at a shrunken mummy in a glass case.

For a time the reader does not really know what to
make of this portentous description of Enoch's enslave-
ment to his wise blood. In a way Enoch's inner life, as it
were, seems no more ridiculous than Hazel's, and one is
not sure how seriously to take, for instance, the suspense-
ful opening lines of the chapter: "That morning Enoch
Emery knew when he woke up that today the person he

could show it to was going to come. He knew by his blood.
He had wise blood like his daddy." The "it" to be shown,
as it turns out, is the mummy in the museum. On this
particular day the rites are interrupted by Hazel at the
point where Enoch is hiding in the abelia bushes at the
pool; Hazel has lost the trail of the Hawkses and come
to Enoch to get their address. When Enoch sees him coming, he knows that Hazel is the one his blood has in mind
to show the mummy to, and he forces Hazel to go with
him through the rites leading up to the visit to the museum. This they do, and at the museum Hazel is in fact
so strangely struck—we can only guess why—by the face
of the mummified man that he suddenly tears himself
away and runs out of the building, with a frantic Enoch
in pursuit. Outside Hazel throws Enoch down and knocks
him out with a blow on the head with a rock. The final
portentous passage of this central Enoch chapter is, again,
a tonally puzzling one:

> When he [Enoch] came to again, Hazel Motes was gone.
> He lay there a minute. He put his fingers to his forehead
> and then held them in front of his eyes. They were streaked
> with red. He turned his head and saw a drop of blood on
> the ground and as he looked at it, he thought it widened
> like a little spring. He sat straight up, frozen-skinned, and
> put his fingers in it, and very faintly he could hear his
> blood beating, his secret blood, in the center of the city.
>   Then he knew that whatever was expected of him was
> only just beginning.

Enoch's obsessions may be comic and ridiculous, but they
seem real and painful enough to him after all, and the
distinction the novel is trying to develop between the true
quest of Hazel Motes and the false—and therefore merely
comic?—quest of the miserable Enoch, is a distinction a
good many readers have not been able to appreciate. This
has been true in spite of the fact that, as we shall see, the
comedy of Enoch's compulsions is to grow much more
expansive in succeeding chapters.

It may be best to trace the Enoch story through to its
end; this is to take, in a way, an oblique approach to the
central story of Hazel Motes, but the Enoch story helps
explain, as much as anything else, the odd tonal climate
in which Hazel's account is set. As it happens, the Enoch
sections of the book have been only scantily treated elsewhere; they tend to get from critics little more than an
irritable dismissal. Stanley Edgar Hyman, for instance,
though he correctly defines, as it would seem, the wise
blood motif of the book, says curtly that the Enoch story
is "unrelated" to the story of Hazel.[8] But the stories are
certainly related thematically, and clearly the Enoch story
is meant to form a kind of counterpoint to the much more
crucial and serious quest of Hazel Motes. Since, moreover, the Enoch story does loom as large as it does—a full
third of the novel is devoted to it—one must pose the
question of whether the Enoch sub-plot does in fact help
bring into dramatic focus the central tale of Hazel's tortured search for religious truth.

While Hazel is trying to come to terms with the challenge presented by Hawks and also to get his Church
Without Christ started with his own style of street-corner
evangelism, we shift from time to time to Enoch and his
growing conviction that his fate, whatever it is, is about
to overtake him. Chapter 8 begins: "Enoch Emery knew
now that his life would never be the same again, because
the thing that was going to happen to him had started to
happen." It had started in fact, we learn, when he had
shown what was in the glass case to Hazel: "That was a
mystery beyond his understanding, but he knew that what
was going to be expected of him was something awful."
His blood is his most sensitive part, Enoch feels; it knows
more than he does—and suddenly it causes him to start
saving his pay.

8. Stanley Edgar Hyman, *Flannery O'Connor* (Minneapolis,
1966), 14.

Enoch's blood then instructs him to clean up his room, to continue his struggle against the animal world by getting the better of a painted elk over his bed by removing his frame and thereby undressing and "reducing" him, and to paint with gilt the inside of a washstand cabinet, as if to prepare it to receive something of sacred importance. The mechanics of all this are described in dogged and rather over-generous detail, but then comes a spirited passage in which the comedy—indeed what now begins to strike the reader as the almost hysterical comedy—of Enoch's obsession with his wise blood comes unwrapped:

> Enoch never nagged his blood to tell him a thing until it was ready. He wasn't the kind of a boy who grabs at any possibility and runs off, proposing this or that preposterous thing. In a large matter like this, he was always willing to wait for a certainty, and he waited for this one, certain at least that he would know in a few days. Then for about a week his blood was in secret conference with itself every day, only stopping now and then to shout some order at him.
>
> On the following Monday, he was certain when he woke up that today was the day he was going to know on. His blood was rushing around like a woman who cleans up the house after the company has come, and he was surly and rebellious. When he realized that today was the day, he decided not to get up. He didn't want to justify his daddy's blood, he didn't want to be always having to do something that something else wanted him to do, that he didn't know what it was and that was always dangerous.
>
> Naturally, his blood was not going to put up with any attitude like this. He was at the zoo by nine-thirty.

Enoch's blood then sends him to town after work and to the movies. As he comes out of the theater, who should be outside preaching but Hazel Motes, demanding for his church a new jesus "that's all man, without blood to waste . . . one that don't look like any other man so you'll look at him"? Hazel's own blood, we now learn, "has set him free," or so he thinks, and the wise blood theme is—technically at least—here rounded out: " 'Look at me!' Hazel Motes cried, with a tare in his throat, 'and you look at a peaceful man! Peaceful because my blood has set me free. Take counsel from your blood and come into the Church Without Christ and maybe somebody will bring us a new jesus and we'll all be saved by the sight of him!' " Enoch, one can well imagine, is struck absolutely dumb by the knowledge that comes over him, and the nearly mute frenzy of his response is one of the comic peaks of the novel: "An unintelligible sound spluttered out of Enoch. He tried to bellow, but his blood held him back. He whispered, 'Listen here, I got him! I mean I can get him! You know! Him! Him I shown you to. You seen him yourself!' " One can see why a reader is occasionally encountered—often a young reader—who feels for this first and in many ways very wacky novel of O'Connor a special affection. And indeed in the final Enoch chapters we find the comic spirit of Enoch's reporting taking on even greater verve; it is clear, by this time, that the author has begun keenly to enjoy the trials of her slow-witted zoo-keeper. Chapter 11 opens as follows:

> The next morning toward noon a person in a long black raincoat, with a lightish hat pulled down low on his face and the brim of it turned down to meet the turned-up collar of the raincoat, was moving rapidly along certain back streets, close to the walls of the buildings. He was carrying something about the size of a baby, wrapped up in news-papers, and he carried a dark umbrella too. . . . He had on a pair of dark glasses and a black beard which a keen ob-server would have said was not a natural growth but was pinned onto his hat on either side with safety pins.

Enoch has come to deliver the new jesus to Hazel Motes! Before he gets to Hazel's roominghouse (where Hazel is, by this time, lying ill in mind and body with his failed evangelism, and is suffering the help and comfort of Sabbath Hawks), Enoch has to endure a humiliating en-counter with the man dressed up in a gorilla suit to pro-mote a movie; and Enoch at first makes the Enoch-like mistake of taking the man for a real ape. Arriving at

Hazel's, the discouraged Enoch just wants to get the new jesus off his hands. He finds Hazel asleep and leaves the mummy with Sabbath Hawks, whose daddy has taken flight while she stayed on to woo unhappy Hazel.

By this time the new jesus, whose face has horrified Hazel in the museum much earlier on, has grown to be too visible a part of the novel for there to be any doubt but that we are being invited to give it some kind of special reading. It seems to me that we are meant to see it as a grim and horrifying symbol, if a funny and absurd one, of the whole succession of false gods that modern man—with what awful stupidity, the book is telling us—continues to invent to replace the one true Jesus. When Sabbath opens the package in which the small mummy is wrapped, even she is momentarily stunned; yet there is something about him that is familiar: "She had never known anyone who looked like him before, but there was something in him of everyone she had ever known, as if they had all been rolled into one person and killed and shrunk and dried." Our false gods are, more than anything else, merely ourselves, our own shrunken, dried up, and above all, mortal—no matter how we try to escape it—selves. Slowly Sabbath—being, after all, the very essence of evil, if we are to believe her herself—begins to fondle and love the new jesus. "Well I declare," she murmurs, "you're right cute, ain't you?" And she finds that his head fits exactly into the hollow of her shoulder. "Who's your momma and daddy?" she asks.

A little later, as Hazel is packing his things to get out of town, he looks up to see Sabbath standing in the door with the new jesus. She says, "Call me momma now." At first Hazel is rendered quite speechless by the sight of Sabbath and her "baby"—it is one of the quirks of the story that Hazel never knows what the reader knows of where it came from. Sabbath says, "Ask your daddy yonder where he was running off to—sick as he is? . . . Ask him isn't he going to take you and me with him!"

Hazel grabs the mummy and hurls it against the wall; it bursts open, and he throws it down the fire escape. Sabbath says she has always known he was bad, "mean enough to slam a baby against a wall," and didn't want anything but Jesus! The reader is in a position to relish the irony that "She's right, it's true!" Hazel only answers, perhaps too grandly, "I don't want nothing but the truth!" He tells Sabbath that he's going to some other city to preach the Church Without Christ, but his chronic cough comes on him again, and he tumbles back into bed, saying that first he has to get some more sleep. The chapter ends with Sabbath's memorable reply: "You ain't going to get none."

Now the free-wheeling comedy of this chapter— Enoch's delivery of the new jesus interrupted by his ordeal with the gorilla, and Sabbath's mock-motherly adoption of it as her "baby"—is in itself diverting enough. But the problem is, and generally conceived this is one of the continuing problems of the novel, that set into this highly farcical episode is a scene of an entirely different order, in which, if it is really to register with the reader, he must empty himself of those assumptions about the spirit of the tale which have made it possible for him to enjoy the broad burlesque of the toylike figures of Enoch and Sabbath.

The scene I am referring to is the one in which we see Hazel alone in his room just before Sabbath comes in with the new jesus. This passage opens with a paragraph that might have been lifted out of the most cautious realistic novel; we get, in fact, a clearer view here of Hazel's exact state of mind at a given moment than we do anywhere else in the book. That paragraph should be looked at, I think, in full:

> Hazel had already been jolted awake when the front door slammed behind Enoch Emery. He had sat up and seeing she was not in the room, he had jumped up and begun to put on his clothes. He had one thought in mind and it had

come to him, like his decision to buy a car, out of his sleep
and without any indication of it beforehand: he was going
to move immediately to some other city and preach the
Church Without Christ where they had never heard of it.
He would get another room there and another woman and
make a new start with nothing on his mind. The entire
possibility of this came from the advantage of having a car
—of having something that moved fast, in privacy, to the
place you wanted to be. He looked out the window at the
Essex. It sat high and square in the pouring rain. He didn't
notice the rain, only the car; if asked he would not have
been able to say that it was raining. He was charged with
energy and he left the window and finished putting on his
clothes. Earlier that morning, when he had waked up for
the first time, he had felt as if he were about to be caught
by a complete consumption in his chest; it had seemed to be
growing hollow all night and yawning underneath him, and
he had kept hearing his coughs as if they came from a distance. After a while he had been sucked down into a
strengthless sleep, but he had waked up with this plan,
and with the energy to carry it out right away.

Such details as we see here—"He didn't notice the rain,
only the car; if asked he would not have been able to say
that it was raining" or "he had been sucked down into
a strengthless sleep," as grateful as we are for them in
respect to our desire to come closer to this queer Hazel—
are still blurred for being clearly out of keeping with
the spirit in which the adjacent scenes are being reported.

As Hazel packs, he runs across his mother's old Bible
and her reading glasses. These items are religious relics
of a kind; we know that they connote for him the fierce
Christianity in which he was brought up. Thus the act
in which he puts on the glasses and, looking in the mirror,
seems to see himself through his mother's eyes is surely
meant to be a very serious sign to the reader of how far
he has yet to go in escaping "the mad stinking figure
of Christ" that, using again the words of the O'Connor
preface, "moves from tree to tree in the back of his
mind." When, therefore, Sabbath Hawks, at the end of
this sequence and of the chapter, suddenly reappears

cuddling Enoch's stolen mummy, the tonal problem which so often disfigures the O'Connor work rears once more an ugly head. For surely, as a frame for the religious ordeal of Hazel Motes that we are being asked to take with bitter seriousness and as a "matter of life and death," the crazy shenanigans of the cartoon-like figures of Sabbath and Enoch are quite wrong. If one is to try to credit these figures at all as images of real people, one has to see them as simply insane, as one early reviewer has in fact done—yet that hardly seems to be the point. The point seems to be that these figures, this surreal world of mere grotesques, represents in some serious way the kind of non-believing world that the modern Christian pilgrim must move through and beyond in order to reach that precious truth found only in Christ.

But even as strictly allegorical figures—and the novel has seldom been about to make much use of such characters—these figures still seem woefully misconceived, for they cannot be said even to represent anything that is very real in normal experience. Miss O'Connor's reply to such a charge, one can be sure, would have been to say that that is the measure of the distance between us, that if we could only see our lives as they really are, we would see how much truth these grossly stylized portraits hold. But our reply would have to be that it is precisely the business of the work of art to bring us to such a realization, rather than simply assaulting us, by the use of such witches' dolls as the *Wise Blood* grotesques, with our blindness and stupidity.

Thus one of the failures at the core of the book lies in the conflicting styles of characterization; it is a problem from which we get almost no relief until, as we shall see shortly, the excellent final scenes of the story. And this problem is again one that directly issues from O'Connor's unusually queer view of human life. O'Connor's true seeker after truth—that is, the person obsessed with the question of whether Jesus lived and died for mankind—

is conceived in a very different way from all other human
beings that cohabit with him this miserable way-station,
the earth. Even the truth-seeker is in many ways ridiculous; human life is above all ridiculous, for the good, she
liked to insist, is something that in humans is "under
construction." But the non-seekers, those doomed individuals whose lives are all equally meaningless, tend to
be reduced to simple cartoons.

This major gap in the O'Connor psychology—it is, in
fact, more an abyss—must be accepted as one of her chief
limitations as a writer; of the ordinary, unsaved and
unsanctified people of the world—and they constitute
after all, she would be the first to agree, the great mass
of society—it is no exaggeration to say that she had a
very meager understanding. A reader, I think, will often
feel in reading O'Connor that for all his own dim com-
prehension of the religious mind (which he brings as his
handicap to the O'Connor works), this writer's compre-
hension of his own mind is far dimmer. Even in her second and much better novel, *The Violent Bear It Away,*
this failure in her perception of the unbelieving world
continued to do damage. She made a much more serious
attempt in that book to balance the conflict between the
religious and non-religious points of view, to set on the
other end of the scale from obsessive religiosity something other than paper dolls and cartoons. Thus we have
the atheist social worker Rayber—a much more plausible
character than any of the secular figures in *Wise Blood,*
but still not wholly satisfactory, as many readers have
been quick to point out.[9]

But to return to Enoch Emery, he is, then, part and
parcel of that unreligious other world that Hazel Motes
tries and triumphantly fails to make his own. As sug-

9. See, for instance, Frank J. Warnke's review of *The Violent
Bear It Away* in *New Republic,* CXLII (March 14, 1960), 18; also
Richard Gilman's review of *Mystery and Manners,* "On Flannery
O'Connor," *New York Review of Books,* VIII (August 21, 1969).

gested earlier, it has been disconcerting for many readers that the stories of Hazel and Enoch do not really converge, on the narrative level, after the tussle outside the museum (that Hazel is never even aware, as far as we know, that Sabbath's "baby" is Enoch's new jesus, the museum mummy) ; that Enoch simply drops out of the book dressed up in a gorilla suit himself and terrorizing a courting couple on a hillside overlooking the city; that, in other words, we never get the final revelation about this character that the novel has seemed to be leading us to. Yet in a sense the final gorilla-suit scene does constitute a kind of logical climax to Enoch's wild pursuit of the fate his wise blood has in mind for him.

The final Enoch chapter opens with an account of Enoch's expectation that the new jesus is "going to do something for him in return for his services"; some reward will come his way: "He wanted to better his condition until it was the best. He wanted to be THE young man of the future, like the ones in the insurance ads. He wanted, someday, to see a line of people waiting [as they had waited for the fake gorilla outside the theater], to shake his hand." Thus his blood directs him on another—for the reader rather dull—tour of the city and finally to another theater where Gonga the Gorilla is promoting his movie. After the ceremonies, Enoch steals into the fake gorilla's van, and as it moves out of the city and into the countryside, we hear thumping noises inside and then see a figure, clutching some garments, slip out of the back of the van as it stops at a crossing. In the dark the figure takes off his clothes and buries them, though burying his clothes, the author tells us outright, "was not a symbol to him of burying his former self; he only knew he wouldn't need them any more." He dons the ape suit, and for a time after he gets the costume fastened and adjusted, he—or rather "it," as the narrator now refers to him—stands quite still. Then, in the two final paragraphs of the chapter, we see the last of Enoch as he undergoes some kind of inner transformation to gorilla. His ambivalent fascination for all the animals he has encountered, the animals at the zoo as well as the painted elk and the fake gorilla, now comes clear. It surely is the author's intention to show that this instinct, this wise blood, of Enoch's, which compels him to certain actions against his will just as Hazel's instinct does him, is the crazed, defective relic of what should be in man the religious instinct. In its modern diseased form, this instinct takes one not to rebirth in Christ, to renewal as a being closer to the angels, but comically down instead of up—to rebirth as a lower animal. And certainly the gross animalism of the whole book, all the mercilessly animalistic descriptions of the faces and actions of the people of the novel, is here crowned:

> For a time after this, it [Enoch in the gorilla suit] stood very still and didn't do anything. Then it began to growl and beat its chest; it jumped up and down and flung its arms and thrust its head forward. The growls were thin and uncertain at first but they grew louder after a second. They became low and poisonous, louder again, low and poisonous again; they stopped altogether. The figure extended its hand, clutched nothing, and shook its arm vigorously; it withdrew the arm, extended it again, clutched nothing and shook. It repeated this four or five times. Then it picked up the pointed stick and placed it at a cocky angle under its arm and left the woods for the highway. No gorilla in existence, whether in the jungles of Africa or California, or in New York City in the finest apartment in the world, was happier at that moment than this one, whose god had finally rewarded it.

And the final image we have of Enoch, sitting at the end of his quest in an ape suit on a hill overlooking the city, is a prefiguration of the image we will shortly have of Hazel Motes, when his own desperate quest has come to an end. When Hazel's old Essex, the sacred home of his anti-Jesus ministry, is pushed over the cliff by the policeman, Hazel too sits down at the edge of a cliff, his face reflecting "the entire distance that extended from his

eyes to the blank gray sky that went on, depth after
depth, into space." The reader senses that Hazel is at long
last overcome with the enormous failure of his attempt
to escape Christ into disbelief and that the wrecking of
the car is to be seen as an act of grace, so that in a sense
Hazel's god—or simply God—has rewarded *him*.

Thus I think it is really not very difficult to see, once
the details are sorted out, how O'Connor was attempting
to use the Enoch Emery parable (if one may use that
term) : to see, that is, how the story is meant to operate
as a kind of parody of the religious search of Hazel Motes.
The argument of the parable is not at all as coherent,
however, as it can be made to seem by lifting out the
pithiest passages, as I have done here. Nor is this story,
even when one understands what is going on, really very
successful in lending force—in making more intelligible,
impressive, or interesting—Hazel's reconversion. This is
the case partly because the analogy is far too deeply
buried under the very broad, stubbornly burlesque man-
ner of the account, but also because even given the broad
burlesque, the tracks of the two stories do not touch more
dramatically at more points. "Without God man is no
better than an animal" is the text of the Enoch tale, and
it is surely an understatement to say that the novel does
not argue this text very effectively. There are no points
in the story where, somehow, let us say, against our
reasoned judgment, we get a glimpse of the truth that
might lie in such a text—nothing in the portrait of Enoch
Emery to slyly or cunningly bring home to us in what
way Enoch's comedy is in essence the comedy of modern
man, ridiculously driven, by the diseased shred of religious sense left him, to a wild, insane search for sheer
animalistic existence.

### 3

Though one could certainly begin with other narrative
strands of the novel just as well, once one understands

what the author is saying through the ordeal of Enoch Emery, *Wise Blood* poses no significant problems of interpretation. Hazel Motes's sermons, for instance, as he preaches his Church Without Christ on the Taulkinham street corners, are clearly meant to state the world view of the godless in such bald, severe terms as to make their essential absurdity seem plain. But curiously, what often happens is that Hazel's statements, even as parodistic as they are intended to be, ring much truer than they ought to: "I preach there are all kinds of truth, your truth and somebody else's, but behind all of them, there's only one truth and that is that there's no truth. . . . No truth behind all truths is what I and this church preach!" And surely the failure of the parody here, the odd ineffectuality of the argument by ridicule, simply measures, once more, the distance between the religious and non-religious views of life. A very large part of modern Christian narrative literature consists—the work of François Mauriac, for instance, consists almost entirely—of story after story meant dramatically to expose the ugliness and absurdity of human life in and of itself; one is told, over and over again, of the futility of all merely human endeavor—of work, of love, even of art. And what is particularly annoying, both in Mauriac and O'Connor, is that one is told all this as if it were an argument for Christian belief.

But in any case, at the beginning of *Wise Blood*, Hazel Motes is shown as a man trying to overcome a deeply fixed, seemingly in-born, contempt for the worldly life. He makes a desperate attempt to thrust himself into the normal round of everyday Taulkinham life; he acquires a woman, a car, and a new suit of clothes, but all these efforts comically misfire sooner or later, and his hollow boasts about his escape from Jesus into the world are the occasion for some of the novel's best lines. "What do I need with Jesus?" he says, "I got Leora Watts"; and of the dilapidated old Essex, he says, "A man with a good car don't need to be justified." But no matter how much violence Hazel does to the Christian doctrine he was reared in, nothing is clearer than that he is different from normal people and will always be seen by them as a freak. As *Wise Blood* opens, we see Hazel on the train to Taulkinham. Our first view of him, just as our last at the close of the book, we get through the eyes of a middle-aged matron who is, to use the folk expression, as ordinary as they come. The vivid juxtaposition between Hazel and these eminently normal and sensible matrons is one of the things that make the opening and closing chapters the stronger parts of the book. We are told that to Mrs. Wally Bee Hitchcock, Hazel's traveling companion and a nearly exact prototype for the succession of middle-aged women who will figure more and more prominently in the short stories, Hazel "didn't look . . . much over twenty, but he had a stiff broad-brimmed hat on his lap, a hat that an elderly preacher would wear. His suit was a glaring blue and the price tag [$11.95] was still stapled on the sleeve of it." Hazel has "a nose like a shrike's bill," his face is fixed in the fierce stare we are reminded of over and over again through the novel, and it is the strange intensity of his eyes, "the color of pecan shells and set in deep sockets," that fascinates Wally Bee Hitchcock, as well as nearly everyone else Hazel will encounter. Exactly like the landlady, whom we last see peering intently into Hazel's dead face at the end of the book, Mrs. Hitchcock finds herself bending closer and closer to those intriguing eyes: "Their settings were so deep that they seemed, to her, almost like passages leading somewhere and she leaned half-way across the space that separated the two seats, trying to see into them." Thus is established what is perhaps the most skillfully developed theme of the book, the vision-blindness theme, which O'Connor repeatedly uses to point up the conflicting views of the world of Hazel and the godless people around him. The fake blindness of the street preacher Hawks works one of the important variations on this theme, but its major

expansion comes in the last chapter after Hazel succeeds
—where Hawks had failed, years ago—in putting out his
eyes with lime as an act of faith and of penance.

On the train we learn that Hazel believes he has some
strange mission in Taulkinham, that he plans "to do some
things he's never done before"—we do not know exactly
what. Hazel has just gotten out of the army, where, the
narrator tells us, he has learned his anti-Christianity.
His mates told him he had no soul: "He took a long time
to believe them because he wanted to believe them. All
he wanted was to believe them and get rid of it [his
soul] once and for all, and he saw the opportunity here
to get rid of it without corruption, to be converted to
nothing instead of evil."

The human scene on the train seems much more real
than the world of hideous evil that Hazel will step into
in Taulkinham, but even here the dire animalism of the
novel is being primed; people tend to be likened to birds
—they are said to dress like parrots, to move like crows,
to wear the expressions of game birds. Two rapid exchanges between Hazel and individuals on the train are
markedly effective in reminding us what an absurd figure
a religious zealot cuts today in the world's eye. At one
point Hazel roughly interrupts Mrs. Hitchcock's rambling monologue about her relations to say: "I reckon
you think you been redeemed." She blushes and replies
that yes, life is an inspiration. In the diner Hazel says
to one of his smart young table-mates: "Do you think I
believe in Jesus? . . . Well I wouldn't even if He existed.
Even if He was on this train." "Who said you had to?"
the girl replies, "in a poisonous Eastern accent."

But what in this first chapter draws the reader close
to Hazel, in spite of his queerness, what makes it possible
for the reader to watch his struggle with something almost like sympathy, is the nature of the picture we get
of him as a boy. We learn that after Hazel's release from
the army, he had gone straight back home to his country

village Eastrod. But his parents had died years ago, and now he finds the village deserted and his old house in ruins. Eastrod, and in fact everything it represents as the primal, natural, and therefore religious home, has simply vanished. This queer disappearance is reflected for Hazel very acutely by the fact that though he recognizes a porter on the train as a Negro from Eastrod, the porter insists he has never heard of it and is from Chicago. Where is Eastrod? is the question the novel is posing. Where is man's true religious home?

One of Hazel's most vivid memories of home is of his preacher grandfather, "a waspish old man who had ridden over three counties with Jesus hidden in his head like a stinger." Hazel had always wanted to be a preacher too (at the same time that he was scared of Jesus and wanted to avoid him), and when the army called him he "had thought at first he would shoot his foot and not go": "He was going to be a preacher like his grandfather and a preacher can always do without a foot. A preacher's power is in his neck and tongue and arm. His grandfather had traveled three counties in a Ford automobile. Every fourth Saturday he had driven into Eastrod as if he were just in time to save them all from Hell, and he was shouting before he had the car door open." Hazel is terrified of the Jesus his granddaddy evokes, bellowing from the nose of his old Ford (just as Hazel is to do—though with a very contrary doctrine—from the top of his old Essex) ; and the granddaddy liked to point to his small dirty grandson as an example of a Christian soul whom Jesus would never let go, saying Jesus would chase him over the waters of sin, Jesus "would have him in the end." And of course Jesus does.

Throughout the O'Connor fiction the fact of mortality is kept constantly before us; there are constant allusions to death and dying, often in an admonitory tone, and of course many vivid depictions of death. It is typical of O'Connor that she should have Hazel, even at the hopeful beginning of his adventure into disbelief, oppressed by thoughts of mortality. As he lies in his train berth on the way to Taulkinham, the closed-in, coffin-like aspect of his berth brings back stark memories of the deaths of his mother, father, and grandfather; what he remembers best is the way in which each one seemed to struggle— with what intensity!—against death and yet was overcome.

The final episode from Eastrod days is told in the second chapter, as Hazel's reflection as he lies with his first woman, the prostitute Leora Watts, whose telephone number he has copied from a toilet wall in the train station. This is one of the most artful passages of the book, perhaps the most affecting except for Hazel's death at the end. It is an account of Hazel's guilt before his mother for having sneaked into a sex show at a carnival. In one rapid exchange at the end of the passage, it captures with wonderful concision the radical ambivalence towards Christ that will mark, more than any other single quality, Hazel as a man. "Jesus died to redeem you," his mother says, as she boxes his head for what he has done, and though Hazel is deeply ashamed and later punishes himself by wearing rocks in his shoes, he says, "I never ast him."

As a reader rereads such passages as these, he may find himself wishing that there were more such moments in *Wise Blood,* and indeed in the O'Connor fiction in general. In short, one would wish to be more involved in Hazel's fate than the novel generally allows one to be. It is almost an understatement to say that one cannot help but feel that particularly in this queerest of her books the reader is overdistanced from the experience of the characters. Still, this wide distancing seems to be a deliberate tactic on the part of the author, and of course we must persist in trying to accept, and assess, the book on its own terms. And yet—what are its terms? In a sense it is true that what the reader constantly strives to achieve in O'Connor books—a feeling for the humanity of the characters that transcends questions of conscious belief, a reaffirmation of his sense that there is a wide range of belief within which we can still respond to a character as a man or woman—is exactly the kind of liberal feeling towards belief that O'Connor means to attack; and part of her means of doing so is to deny the reader the satisfaction of an emotional, non-ideological response. But to make this complaint is to reveal ourselves as those very readers who according to O'Connor represent so heavy a burden for the religious writer—readers, that is, for whom "moral distinctions are blurred in hazes of compassion."

A writer who could have sympathized with O'Connor's strategy in this regard was Richard Wright. After writing the stories of *Uncle Tom's Children,* Wright came to feel that for all his white readers' compassion for the heartrending fates of the black Mississippi peasants of those stories, he had not really succeeded in forcing readers to a clearer contemplation of the continuing American race war. We know that in *Native Son* he deliberately created a black hero with whom it was much harder for white readers to come to terms emotionally.

Doubtless Miss O'Connor had observed that there are any number of religious characters in traditional novels that the reader loves and admires without being at all swayed by their religious ideas. It was not, I think it is fair to say, compassion for and tolerance of modern Christian zealots that she sought in her books, but—a considerable body of O'Connor criticism notwithstanding— a facing of the issue of Christian belief itself. Probably O'Connor consciously realized, to some extent at least, the danger she risked by what she denied her readers. It meant she had to rely a great deal on the sheer physical vividness with which the characters' strange actions could be evoked, as well as the reader's curiosity about

the bizarre paths these weird characters' compulsions
would lead them into and about the nature of the compulsions themselves.

Now all of this is not to say that there are not places
in the O'Connor fiction where her guard in this respect
was, so to speak, let down. Two of the stories we have
already mentioned stand out as rather high achievements
in a more traditional style: "The River," about a small
boy's baptism in a river and his subsequent drowning,
and "The Artificial Nigger," about an old man's taking
his grandson on his first trip to the city. In the latter it
is possible, for instance, to feel sympathy for the old
man's gentle religiosity—to feel that it ennobles his life
and the crucial relationship with his grandson. The tenor
of this story is quite different from what she seemed to
be striving for in the main body of her work, and it is
odd to read that it was one of her favorites. As we shall
see in the next chapter, it is in another tale about an old
man and a boy, in the novel *The Violent Bear It Away*,
that we get the most affectionate, and probably the most
satisfying, treatment of character—that is, of old Tarwater. But taking the four books as a whole, tonally these
parts of her work are certainly the exception, not the
rule.

One thing that O'Connor did not hit upon in *Wise
Blood* that was to profit her a great deal in *The Violent
Bear It Away*, was some narrative tool to drive the action
forward, such as the charge laid on young Tarwater by
his uncle at his uncle's death: that is, the charge to carry
on the uncle's prophecy after his death by baptizing the
retarded child Bishop. In *Wise Blood* the action does not
have the kind of continuity and cohesion that the charge
to Tarwater makes possible in *The Violent Bear It Away*;
and though *Wise Blood* is written with just as fierce an
intensity as *The Violent Bear It Away*, it is, in part, the
intense, prophetic style of *Wise Blood* that we come to

distrust as we lose confidence in the writer to provide the completions for the action that her portentous prose seems to promise.

One of the devices she tried to use, but somehow not to maximum effect, was the challenge presented to Hazel's disbelief by the street preacher Hawks. Hawks claims, it will be recalled, to have blinded himself years ago at a revival, as an act of faith; what Hazel wants to find out is whether he really did so, for his feeling seems to be that if a man could blind himself for Jesus, then Jesus may really exist. Though Hawks remains too inert an antagonist for this direction of the story to be very richly extended, there is one brief scene which must be singled out for the hauntingly vivid image it creates; I am referring to the scene in which Hazel steals into Hawks's room during the night as he is sleeping and, holding a lighted match over the old man's face, peers into it to try to see whether he is actually blind.

> After a while when he had tried the wire five or six different ways, there was a slight click in the lock [of Hawks's door]. He stood up, trembling, and opened the door. His breath came short and his heart was palpitating as if he had run all the way here from a great distance. He stood just inside the room until his eyes got accustomed to the darkness and then he moved slowly over to the iron bed and stood there. Hawks was lying across it. His head was hanging over the edge. Haze squatted down by him and struck a match close to his face and he opened his eyes. The two sets of eyes looked at each other as long as the match lasted; Haze's expression seemed to open onto a deeper blankness and reflect something and then close again.
> "Now you can get out," Hawks said in a short thick voice, "now you can leave me alone," and he made a jab at the face over him without touching it. It moved back, expressionless under the white hat, and was gone in a second.

One other dramatic peak of the novel, Hazel's killing of the false prophet, demands comment before we move to the final scene. Solace Layfield has been hired to emulate Hazel's preaching style by an ex-radio preacher

Hoover Shoats, who wants to horn in on what he sees as
Hazel's new-jesus racket. ("There's no such thing as any
new jesus," Hazel tries to tell him; "that ain't nothing but
a way to say something." And Shoats's irritable reply is
a nice one: "That's the trouble with you innerleckshuls,
you don't never have nothing to show for what you're
saying.") Shoats has Layfield dress up to look like Hazel
and get up on the nose of his car just as Hazel does and
preach Hazel's doctrine. Hazel discovers what Layfield is
doing and follows him home one night, wrecks his car,
and runs him down.

This is one of the most trying episodes for the reader
and harks back to the massacre scene in "A Good Man Is
Hard to Find." One knows exactly what this scene is
meant to do: to put the case for Hazel's super-integrity—
for the earnestness of his pursuit—in the most dramatic,
indeed the most outrageous, terms possible; nor is one
likely to miss here the essential irony: Hazel kills Layfield, not because he is an enemy of the truth as Hazel sees
it—that is, of the Church Without Christ—but because
he preaches the truth without believing in it!

Now the trouble is that the narrator asks for respect
for Hazel's dilemma here—if she does not ask for approval of the deed exactly, she certainly asks for understanding, I think perhaps even for pity—but she makes
an extended comic point of denying any to Hazel's victim.
Layfield is breezily referred to, for instance, as the
Prophet, yet his death is described in sharp and painful
detail. How reconcile such details as these? a) "[Layfield]
had consumption and a wife and six children and being a
prophet was as much work as he wanted to do"; b) "A lot
of blood was coming out of him and forming a puddle
around his head. He was motionless all but for one finger
that moved up and down in front of his face as if he were
marking time with it. Haze poked his toe in his side and
he wheezed for a second and then was quiet." The Prophet
dies choking on his own blood, saying "Jesus hep me."

Thus—how else to sum it up?—O'Connor throws down another smirking challenge to the weak-hearted reader, that hazy-minded "compassionate" reader whom the amoral, irreligious modern novel has helped to create. It is strange to have to speak so harshly of this particular passage—it probably marks the lowest point in the reader's struggle to see through to the beauty and significance of Hazel's quest—for it is literally on the next page following this passage that we begin a part of the novel that must be spoken of in very different terms.

After Hazel kills the false prophet, he makes his final decision to move to another city and start his ministry over again. On his way out of Taulkinham the next morning he stops at a gas station to have the needs of the old Essex attended to. The Essex clearly represents to him all the satisfactions and achievements of the worldly existence in which a godless man like himself must find such solace as he can. "Nobody with a good car needs to be justified," we have heard him insist; and here he is still explaining to the station attendant that it is not "right to believe anything you can't see or hold in your hands or test with your teeth." The attendant gives Haze a full report on the car's doomed condition, but Haze says, "Listen, this car is just beginning its life. A lightening bolt couldn't stop it!"

Hazel gets only five miles out of town before he is stopped by a policeman, who takes a sudden dislike to Hazel's face and wrecks the Essex by shoving it off an embankment. The drama of this remarkable action and Hazel's response to it is all the more intensely felt because of the guarded, understated way in which it is told. We then get an eerie view of the final winding down of the conflict in Hazel's mind as he sits numbly on the edge of the embankment and looks not so much at the ruined old car, but beyond into the "blank gray sky that went on, depth after depth, into space."

Hazel walks back to Taulkinham, and on his way he

buys a bucket of lime. And at this point the book's tonal
problems quite wonderfully evanesce. There is little in any
of O'Connor's books that is tonally more nearly perfect
than the delicate description of Hazel's self-blinding that
follows. What is kept in remarkable balance here is the
reader's sense, on the one hand, of Motes as a religious
monomaniac and his sense, on the other hand, of the
deadly significance for Hazel himself of what he does:

> When he reached the house, he stopped outside on the side-
> walk and opened the sack of lime and poured the bucket half
> full of it. Then he went to a water spigot by the front steps
> and filled up the rest of the bucket with water and started
> up the steps. His landlady was sitting on the porch, rocking
> a cat. "What are you going to do with that, Mr. Motes?"
> she asked.
> "Blind myself," he said and went on in the house.
> The landlady sat there for a while longer. She was not a
> woman who felt more violence in one word than in another.
> . . . Still, instead of blinding herself, if she had felt that
> bad, she would have killed herself and she wondered why
> anybody wouldn't do that. . . . Perhaps Mr. Motes was only
> being ugly, for what possible reason could a person have for
> wanting to destroy their sight? . . . It occurred to her sud-
> denly that when she was dead she would be blind too. She
> stared in front of her intensely, facing this for the first
> time. She recalled the phrase, "eternal death," that preach-
> ers used, but she cleared it out of her mind immediately,
> with no more change of expression than the cat. She was
> not religious or morbid, for which every day she thanked
> her lucky stars.

This passage ends the penultimate chapter of the book,
and the final chapter is given over to Hazel's reclusive,
penitent, ascetic life in his room in Mrs. Flood's board-
inghouse. One does not mean to say that there is anything
like an abrupt tonal shift at any point in this area of the
novel. But as the author approaches the final penance and
death of her unlikely hero; as she shuts down the fierce,
devastating, sometimes uproarious assault on godless city
life; as the curtain is pulled over the broad burlesque of

such characters as Enoch Emery and Sabbath Hawks; and as Hazel's heretofore frenetic life enters a new phase of outward quiet and solitude, there is a gradual but more and more perceptible and pleasurable mellowing of the spirit of the tale.

Even though readers have apparently not responded to this final part of the novel, have not pointed it out as the fine writing it is, the strange beauty of it will, I think, be felt by anyone not too oppressed by the weaknesses and frustrations of the rest of the book to reread it with an open mind. One of the most fortunate strokes in this last part of the book is that from the time of Hazel's self-blinding to his death, we see his whole travail through the astonished eyes of Mrs. Flood, the landlady—a character of no importance in the book up until this point—and we are able to feel, not only pity for the plight of Hazel himself, but also for hers. The theme of the whole section is, of course, the vision-blindness theme, physical sight versus spiritual vision, and the landlady's stubborn feeling that the blind man, in spite of his queerness and seeming distractedness, can see something she cannot see is the major subject of the passage. These two characters occupy now one's whole attention. On the stripped screen of the novel they are shown alone together in closely drawn conflict after conflict. It is O'Connor's triumph here to succeed in making the landlady represent, in the most natural and unforced way, the whole normal, secular world—the sceptical world, that is, as it tries to peer, sometimes with uneasy curiosity, into the mystery of religious belief. But we also get, through Hazel's disgust with the landlady's interference in his private world of penance and redemption, a stark view of the way in which the failure of the unbeliever to intuit the existence of a world beyond this world makes him seem to the mystic so childishly, ludicrously blind. The humor here has gentled and receded, but by no means disappeared. One smiles, to be sure, at the landlady's dilemma, at her gross

materialism ("When she found a stream of wealth"—
Hazel's veteran's pension—"she followed it to its source
and before long, it was not distinguishable from her
own."), her irritated sense of being cheated by being shut
out of the blind man's inner world, her shock at Hazel's
outlandish statements and behavior. "Why do you do these
things for?" she says, when she discovers that he is wearing wire under his shirt. And when Hazel says, "I'm not
clean," she says with sublime obtuseness, "You ought to
get you a washwoman." But the landlady is by no means
the most maligned of O'Connor's unreligious characters.
For her there is even hope, for her baffling encounter with
this half-crazy fanatic has brought her by the end of the
novel to the threshold of religious experience.

And what is nicely done here—what one hardly knows
how to account for in such a book—is the moving way in
which the landlady is personally drawn to Hazel. She decides she wants to marry him—at first simply for his
pension, but then (and the reader comes to forget, as she
does, that he is a very young man, so old does he seem
now in experience) for what he knows, even for what he
has suffered. Many passages hereunto could be cited, but
consider this lovely image of the landlady lying in bed at
night thinking of Hazel, sick and blind, abroad in the
winter night. When he had left her house, disgusted by
her pursuit of him, she had "stood at the top of the stairs
for a long time." "He'll be back," she had muttered. "Let
the wind cut into him a little": "That night a driving icy
rain came up and lying in her bed, awake at midnight,
Mrs. Flood, the landlady began to weep. She wanted to
run out into the rain and cold and hunt him and find him
huddled in some half-sheltered place and bring him back
and say, Mr. Motes, Mr. Motes, you can stay here forever,
or the two of us will go where you're going, the two of us
will go."

The better one knows the O'Connor writings, the more
satisfying this final chapter of *Wise Blood* is, for a great

deal of the promise of the O'Connor art is here fulfilled; the drama of the convergence of religious and irreligious minds is, it may be, more fully realized at the end of this often troublesome and exasperating book than it is in any single one of the vaunted short stories. Here O'Connor's comic insight, clearly one of her great gifts, assumes its natural function, enriching the drama of—and clarifying rather than reducing to farce—the conflict that lies at the center of all her work.

But let the final paragraph of the novel speak for itself. Hazel, dying of pneumonia—really, in effect, of self-abuse —is found one night half-conscious in a ditch by two policemen, who finish him off with their billy clubs and take him home to Mrs. Flood's:

> She had never observed his face more composed and she grabbed his hand and held it to her heart. It was resistless and dry. The outline of a skull was plain under his skin and the deep burned eye sockets seemed to lead into the dark tunnel where he had disappeared. She leaned closer and closer to his face, looking deep into them, trying to see how she had been cheated or what had cheated her, but she couldn't see anything. She shut her eyes and saw the pin point of light but so far away that she could not hold it steady in her mind. She felt as if she were blocked at the entrance of something. She sat staring with her eyes shut, into his eyes, and felt as if she had finally got to the beginning of something she couldn't begin, and she saw him moving farther and farther away, farther and farther into the darkness until he was the pin point of light.

### 4

To this discussion of *Wise Blood* a footnote remains to be added regarding O'Connor's earliest published fiction. This work consists of seven fictional pieces published during the six years before the appearance of *Wise Blood* in 1952. (For the location of these early writings I am indebted to Melvin Friedman's and Lewis Lawson's excellent O'Connor bibliographies in the O'Connor critical

compendium *The Added Dimension.*[10]) Four of these
pieces are short stories; they include the story "The
Train" from which the idea for *Wise Blood* originally
came. And three are excerpts from "a novel in progress"
—that is, *Wise Blood*; they were lifted out of whatever
draft of the novel she was working on at the time and give
us a certain amount of information about the course of
the book's development.

The first three of these early pieces we can be reason-
ably sure she wrote before she began *Wise Blood,* and
what is interesting about them is that they differ very
markedly in tone from *Wise Blood* and all her subsequent
work. The very first story, "The Geranium," came out
when she was just twenty-one and would have to have
been written while she was still an undergraduate at the
state women's college in Milledgeville, Georgia, or early in
her first year at the University of Iowa (where she attended the Writer's Workshop and earned a Master of
Fine Arts degree).

"The Geranium" is the story of an old man's transplan-
tation from a southern country town to his married daug-
ter's New York apartment. Old Dudley is being forced to

10. Melvin J. Friedman and Lewis A. Lawson, eds., *The Added
Dimension* (New York, 1966).
Just after I completed this discussion of O'Connor's pre-*Wise
Blood* stories, three previously unpublished stories became avail-
able in *The Complete Stories of Flannery O'Connor* (New York,
1971). The three new stories ("The Barber," "Wildcat," and "The
Crop") were submitted by O'Connor for her M.A. thesis at the
University of Iowa along with the three early stories, all published
in journals before *Wise Blood,* which I examine herein: "The
Geranium," "The Capture" (originally titled "The Turkey"), and
"The Train."
Despite the appearance of these additional stories, it seems un-
necessary to alter my discussion of the early stories actually published, for my main argument—that the early work differs markedly
in tone from *Wise Blood* and all subsequent work—is not by any
means thrown into question by the three added stories, which are
all conventionally mild and friendly pieces with none of the prophetic fierceness of *Wise Blood.*

live on his daughter and son-in-law's strained charity, and
he is suffering the predictable torments—often vividly
described—of country people in the city:

> They [Old Dudley and his daughter] went on an overhead
> train too. She called it an "El." They had to go up on a
> high platform to catch it. Old Dudley looked over the rail
> and could see the people rushing and the automobiles rush-
> ing under him. He felt sick. He put one hand on the rail
> and sank down on the wooden floor of the platform. The
> daughter screamed and pulled him over from the edge. "Do
> you want to fall off and kill yourself?" she shouted.
> Through a crack in the boards he could see the cars swim-
> ming in the street. "I don't care," he murmured, "I don't
> care if I do or not."
> "Come on," she said, "you'll feel better when we get
> home."
> "Home?" he repeated. The cars moved in a rhythm below
> him.
> "Come on," she said, "here it comes; we've just got time
> to make it." They'd just had time to make all of them.
> They made that one. They came back to the building and
> the apartment. The apartment was too tight. There was no
> place to be where there wasn't somebody else. The kitchen
> opened into the bathroom and the bathroom opened into
> everything else and you were always where you started
> from.

Worse really comes to worse when a Negro moves in next
door and patronizes Dudley in the hall. Dudley thinks of
himself as having come from "a good place" where "such
as that couldn't be," and now he feels that he is "trapped
in this place where niggers could call you 'old-timer.'"
O'Connor attempts to give shape to the story by opening
and closing it with accounts of the old man's obsession
with a sickly potted geranium which is put out each day
on a neighbor's window ledge. Dudley is contemptuous of
the geranium—"Ours [at home] are sho nuff geraniums,"
he thinks to himself, "not any er this pale pink business
with green, paper bows"; but at least it is alive and it
reminds him of home, and of course its struggle to live

in its artificial environment is similar to Dudley's own.

The story ends almost too pathetically as Dudley sinks weeping in his chair after his humiliating encounter with the Negro and suddenly realizes that the geranium is missing from its place on the ledge. When he asks its owner across the way what happened to it, this ill-tempered man tells him that the geranium was knocked off the ledge into the alley, and he gives Dudley a mean-Yankee tongue-lashing for not minding his own business.

"The Capture," published in *Mademoiselle* about two years after the appearance of "The Geranium," concerns a young boy's attempt to bring home from the woods a wild turkey. The narration consists almost entirely of the boy's stream of thought, generally in his own idiom. Ruller discovers the turkey while he is pretending to round up outlaws, and dreaming of walking proudly home with it slung over his shoulder, he chases it, but it gets away. He is so angry and disappointed at losing this prize that he does the meanest thing he can think of—he curses:

> "Goddamnit," he said softly. He could feel his face getting hot and his chest thumping all of a sudden inside. "Goddamnit to hell," he said almost inaudibly. He looked over his shoulder but no one was there. . . .
> "Good Father, good God, sweep the chicken out the yard," he said and began to giggle. His face was very red. "Our Father Who art in heaven, shoot 'em six and roll 'em seven," he said, giggling again. Boy, his mother'd smack his head in if she could hear him. Goddamnit, she'd smack his goddamn head in. He rolled over in a fit of laughter. Goddamnit, she'd dress him off and wring his goddamn neck like a goddamn chicken.

Suddenly Ruller spies the turkey rolled over dead in a thicket. It seems that some hunter has shot it and lost its trail, and Ruller is overcome by the eerie feeling that God has arranged to have him find the turkey so as to lift his morale and save him from going bad like his cursing, cigarette-smoking brother. "Maybe finding the turkey was a sign. Maybe God wanted him to be a preacher. He thought of Bing Crosby and Spencer Tracy. He might found a place to stay for boys who were going bad."

As Ruller walks home, his sense of having been chosen by God for this special favor is deepened when he meets a neighborhood beggar woman to whom he can give the dime he has in his pocket as an expression of gratitude for having found the turkey. But just as the radiant Ruller nears his home, three tough boys from the country appear out of nowhere, grab the turkey, and run away with it. Now what is Ruller to think about his special destiny? This is the final paragraph of the story:

> They were in the next block before Ruller moved. Finally, he realized that he could not even see them any longer, they were so far away. He turned toward home, almost creeping. He walked four blocks and then suddenly, noticing that it was dark, he began to run. He ran faster and faster, and as he turned up the road to his house, his heart was running as fast as his legs and he was certain that Something Awful was tearing after him with its arms rigid and its fingers ready to clutch.

One need hardly stop to point out the obvious parallels in this child's religious experience and the religious ordeals of Hazel Motes and of Tarwater in *The Violent Bear It Away*; the differences, on the other hand, between this and later works are, as we shall see, much more interesting; and on this subject one may interpose a few lines from the note attached to this piece when it was reprinted in 1961 in *Best Stories from Mademoiselle*: "This story shows her [O'Connor's] considerable early talent, with its compassion and ability to build suspense. The view of the world Miss O'Connor presents to her readers in 1960"—note the almost defiant tone of the last clause— "is much more terrifying, although it is still compassionate." [11]

The short story "The Train" appeared in the same year

---

11. Cyrilly Abels and Margarita G. Smith (eds.), *Best Stories from Mademoiselle* (New York, 1961), 343.

as "The Capture," and as we shall see shortly, it is hardly
distinguishable from "The Geranium" and "The Capture"
in its tone and narrative mode.

What is immediately striking about these early stories,
for one who knows O'Connor's later work, is that each
one has a very warmly conceived central character with
whom the reader is closely engaged from the first line of
the story to the last and whose mind is laid completely
and sympathetically open to the reader at every turn of
the story. For a writer, in other words, who is one of the
prime eccentrics of our recent literature, these stories are
amazingly normal stories. The whole human scene as
O'Connor creates it in these early stories is a much more
regular and familiar scene than in the later works—it is
nothing at all like the crazily distorted world of *Wise
Blood*. There are occasionally people who unexpectedly
do mean things—the boys who steal Ruller's turkey, for
instance, and the ill-tempered neighbor of "The Geranium"—but the monsters and grotesques of the later work
are here conspicuously absent. It is a world which (for
good or ill as far as O'Connor's art is concerned) one can
easily accept as real and normal, both in the manners of
southern life portrayed and in the interior lives of the
main characters.

The effects of these stories depend, in other words, on
our being able to take an affectionate interest in the
plights of the main characters and to accept their short-
comings and weaknesses in an easily tolerant spirit—Old
Dudley's racism, for instance, seen from the inside seems
simply amusingly innocent—and to desire their good
fortune and feel pain when things turn out badly for
them. We feel rather unambiguously sorry, within the
limits of "The Geranium" 's modest power to bend us to
its will, for Dudley's continued humiliation and unhap-
piness in the hated New York apartment—sorry when
his hope of making a friend of the young Negro is dashed
and when the geranium is knocked off the ledge.

Now in most of the later O'Connor stories the relationship of reader to character is of course quite different from this. Think of the way in which we perceive and respond to the final fates of such characters as Mrs. May, Sheppard of "The Lame Shall Enter First," or Asbury of "The Enduring Chill." The stories with religious heroes are an exception to almost anything that can be said about the others, but in most of the short stories it seems to be almost the point of the tale that the reader, in spite of his natural inclination to sympathize with individuals caught in such painful situations, be turned more and more against them. One can hardly imagine the author of these early stories making the contemptuous remarks about "compassionate writing" which O'Connor made in later years.

One datum of Miss O'Connor's early life must be mentioned here, even though it turns out to be worth a good deal less than one might at first suppose. It was during the time between the publication of this early short fiction and the appearance of *Wise Blood* in 1952 that Miss O'Connor came down with the disease disseminated lupus, a degenerative and often crippling disease akin to rheumatoid arthritis, that was to take her life at age thirty-nine. One must leave it up to Miss O'Connor's biographers to attempt a full reading of this critical period of her life and her career; yet when one looks at these early pre-illness stories, one can hardly resist leaping to the conclusion that Miss O'Connor's illness explains a great deal about the harshness of her later work. If we reflect on her gallant, almost puzzlingly relaxed acceptance of her condition, to the point that she seems never to have mentioned it, even in letters to close friends,[12] except in a

12. See, for instance, Fitzgerald's references to O'Connor's letters in his introduction to *Everything That Rises Must Converge* and her letters to William Sessions in *The Added Dimension*, 209–25; her unpublished letters to Elizabeth McKee in the O'Connor papers at the Georgia College library in Milledgeville, Georgia, are also interesting on the subject of her illness.

joking way, it is only natural to wonder whether the inevitable pain and frustration of living with such a condition was—while not allowed to disrupt the surface of
her life—driven instead all the more deeply into her work.

I put forth this idea only to say that the evidence does
not really support such a view. If we look more closely
at the record of her writing during the few years preceding her illness, we see that in fact two entirely characteristic excerpts of *Wise Blood* had been published the year
before she came down with the lupus; she became ill in
the fall of 1950 while she was living with the Fitzgeralds
in Connecticut. Fitzgerald tells us that she was typing the
first complete draft of the book when she noticed the
heaviness in her arms that turned out to be the first signs
of the disease. She went home to Georgia, to Emory
Hospital, and she had to put the manuscript aside for
nearly a year while she recuperated from the initial severe
bout of the disease; but during that time the book was
accepted by Harcourt, Brace.[13] When she was able to work
again, and before the final draft was sent to the publisher,
O'Connor made certain stylistic changes suggested by
Caroline Gordon. But in any case the differences between
the two early published excerpts of the book and the novel
as finally published are certainly not differences in the
book's tone or in its bleak and forbidding thesis.

Several years earlier, in the spring of 1948, the seminal
*Wise Blood* story "The Train" had appeared in the
*Sewanee Review*; and the first two excerpts from the
novel-in-progress *Wise Blood* came out the following year
in *Partisan Review*.[14] The first of these, called "The Heart

13. On the early publishing history of *Wise Blood* (it had won
a prize at Rinehart and was to have been published there, but
author and publisher had a falling out over revisions), see Robert
Giroux's introduction to *The Complete Stories*; for the story in
full see the correspondence of O'Connor and Elizabeth McKee in
the Georgia College papers.
14. All the published excerpts from the novels are reprinted in
*The Complete Stories*.

of the Park," is the chapter in which Enoch and Hazel go
through the rites at the zoo leading up to the viewing of
the mummy in the museum; and the second one, "The
Peeler," describes the initial meeting between Hazel,
Enoch, and the Hawkses at the stand of the potato-peeler
man and Hazel's harassment of Hawks and his daughter
as they pass out leaflets on the street. The last excerpt
is much less important, as it did not come out until the
year the novel itself was published: "Enoch and the
Gorilla" combines two late chapters about Enoch's encounters with Gonga at the movie theaters and ends with
Enoch's inner transformation to gorilla. Except for the
welding together of the two chapters and some incidental
cutting that this required, this material is identical to the
final draft of the book.

That at least the early sections of the book had taken
very nearly final shape as early as the beginning of 1949
is attested to by the first excerpt, "The Heart of the Park."
The only changes to be made in this piece were a few
minor deletions of folk idiom in the third-person narration; "The Peeler," and one assumes the whole book, was
also subjected to such changes. A construction such as
"the blind man didn't pay him any mind," for instance,
would be changed to "the blind man didn't pay any attention to him." Here O'Connor was following the advice of
Caroline Gordon. Fitzgerald writes: "One of Caroline's
main points was that the style of the narrator should be
more consistently distinct from the style of the characters,
and I believe that Flannery saw the rightness of this and
learned quickly when and when not to use a kind of indirect discourse in the country idiom she loved." [15] This
distinction is not at all clearly made in the earliest stories
("The Geranium," "The Capture," and "The Train"), and
it is true that her practice was generally in favor of the
distinction in all the work following *Wise Blood*.

15. Fitzgerald's introduction to *Everything That Rises Must Converge*, xviii.

In "The Peeler" one notices one important and interesting difference from the final draft: in this early excerpt the street preacher Hawks is a real blind man and apparently a sincere believer honestly trying to win Hazel back to Christ. In the later draft an ironic dimension to this relationship is supplied by making Hawks's blindness doubtful from the beginning and by showing him as oddly snide and sinister. In *Wise Blood,* for instance, we read: " 'Some preacher has left his mark on you.' the blind man said [to Hazel] with a kind of snicker. 'Did you follow for me to take it off or give you another one?' " The vision-blindness motif was, in fact, strengthened in a number of ways in the final draft.

But I wish now to return to the fact that the differences between these early and late drafts of *Wise Blood* are not nearly so marked as the deep tonal contrast between the original story "The Train" and all the subsequent *Wise Blood* material. In tone "The Train" is very like the other early stories discussed above ("The Geranium" and "The Capture"), and if we look closely at the kinds of changes she made in this story as she reworked and expanded it for the opening of her first novel, we get a glimpse of the author in search of a means of moving away from the mild, warm, predictable mode of this earliest work.

There is nothing particularly strange or fierce about the Hazel we see on his way to Chattanooga in "The Train"; he is simply a lonesome, sensitive, uncertain country boy who feels that everything important in his life has vanished with the virtual disappearance of his native village Eastrod. His sense of loss is deepened by the Negro porter's blanket denial of their common origins—he recognizes the porter as from an Eastrod Negro family, but the porter insists he is from Chicago. Hazel is altogether a much less forbidding character than the Hazel of *Wise Blood,* and this is true partly because there is no mystery about what is taking place in the boy's mind. Early in the story we read, for instance, that "Haze wanted to talk to the porter. What would the porter say when he told him, I'm from Eastrod too? What would he say?" Later, after the porter's denial, Hazel realizes suddenly who he is: "This is Cash's son who ran away; he knows about Eastrod and doesn't want it, he doesn't want to talk about it, he doesn't want to talk about Eastrod." Later, as Hazel is lying in his berth, the top of the berth seems, just as it does in *Wise Blood,* to be closing in on him like the lid of a coffin. One wonders why O'Connor liked this touch so much—are we to assume that with the demise of Eastrod and all that held meaning for him there, Hazel feels that he is dying too? In any case, we are given this explicitly affective stream of the boy's thought:

> The top of the berth was low and curved over. He lay down. The curved top looked like it was not quite closed; it looked like it was closing. . . . He reached up without turning and felt for the button and snapped it and the darkness sank down on him and then faded a little with light from the aisle that came in through the foot of space not closed. He wanted it all dark, he didn't want it diluted. He heard the porter's footsteps coming down the aisle, soft into the rug, coming steadily down, brushing against the green curtains and fading up the other way out of hearing. He was from Eastrod. From Eastrod but he hated it. Cash wouldn't have put any claim on him. He wouldn't have wanted him. He wouldn't have wanted anything that wore a monkey white coat and toted a whiskbroom in his pocket. Cash's clothes had looked like they'd set a while under a rock; and they smelled like a nigger. He thought how they smelled, but he smelled the train. No more gulch niggers in Eastrod. In Eastrod. Turning in the road, he saw in the dark, half-dark, the store boarded and the barn open with the dark free in it, and the smaller house half carted away, the porch gone and no floor in the hall. He had been supposed to go to his sister's in Taulkinham on his last furlough when he came up from the camp in Georgia but he didn't like it in Taulkinham and he had gone back to Eastrod even though he knew how it was: the two families scattered in towns and even the niggers from up and down the road gone into Memphis and Murfreesboro and other places. He had gone back and slept in the house on the floor in the kitchen and a

board had fallen on his head out of the roof and cut his
face. He jumped, feeling the board, and the train jolted and
unjolted and went again.

In *Wise Blood* Hazel's preoccupation with the porter
still forms a major part of the story but is made much
more mysterious. In *Wise Blood* we are given no such passage as the above, showing, from the inside, Hazel's distress with the porter's denial; and in fact we cannot quite
tell why Hazel *does* haunt the porter up and down the
aisles of the train—and we are not even sure that the
porter is in truth the Eastrod Negro Hazel takes him for.
In other words, as O'Connor rewrote "The Train," she
began to move the central character farther and farther
away from the reader—he is moved even farther back, as
I pointed out earlier, in the chapters that follow—so that
he becomes a much stranger and more puzzling character,
an individual whom the reader must constantly struggle
to come to terms with.

While the short story opens with a description of Hazel's thoughts as he begins his trip and continues in such
a way as to allow us to see everything on the train from
his point of view, *Wise Blood* opens, as we saw a few pages
back, with a view of Hazel from the outside—that is, with
Mrs. Wally Bee Hitchcock's impression of his shrike-like
face, cheap clothing, and fiercely staring eyes; and it is
this grim and bizarre exterior of Hazel that is constantly
kept before us in the next few chapters. In the excerpt
published as "The Heart of the Park"—within a year after
"The Train"—we see Hazel, for instance, almost wholly
from the point of view of Enoch Emery, and at critical
moments of the drama we are told, not what is going on
in Hazel's mind, but merely that "his face might have been
cut out of the side of a rock" or that his eyes looked "like
two clean bullet holes." And of course the reader is continually startled and puzzled by his odd and often violent
behavior—his sudden outburst ("I ain't clean") to the

waitress at the Frosty Bottle and later to the caged owl, and his assault on Enoch outside the museum.

But what is even more to the point is that the ordinary country youth of "The Train" is not, as he was to become in *Wise Blood*, a "Jesus-Hog"; in fact the religious element in the village life he knew as a child hardly surfaces here at all. Hazel's memory of his preacher-grandfather and his own desire to be a preacher was added for the novel, so that in "The Train" all of Hazel's explosive remarks to the people on the train—"I reckon you think you been redeemed" and "Do you think I believe in Jesus? . . . Well, I wouldn't even if He existed"—are missing; and Hazel's attitude about his upbringing and toward the people he meets on the train is markedly different. The latter is best pointed up by a single detail: a sentence in "The Train" impossible to imagine in the same sequence in *Wise Blood*. Mrs. Wally Bee Hitchcock (her last name is "Hosen" in "The Train") is the same kind of character in both stories, but in "The Train" she is much more gently treated, and when she sits down next to Hazel and starts talking to him we are told that "Haze was glad to have someone there talking"! It is hardly too much to say that Hazel is glad of scarcely any human encounter in *Wise Blood*.

In all this early fiction, in fact, there is much less satiric abuse than later of the main characters or of the general human scene against which the main action is played, and therefore little foreshadowing of the kind of mean comedy that O'Connor was to become famous for. In "The Train" one notes, along with the fact that even Mrs. Hitchcock-Hosen is spared any real comic abuse, that there are no eastern girls with poisonous voices, no mean stewards to humiliate Hazel in the dining car; nor is there any exchange comparable to the one between Hazel and the porter which ends the first chapter of *Wise Blood* on such a sinister note:

[Hazel] hung there over the top of the berth curtain [terri-
fied by his dream of the top of the berth closing in on him
like the lid of a coffin] and saw the porter at the other end
of the car, a white shape in the darkness, standing there
watching him and not moving.
    "I'm sick!" he called. "I can't be closed up in this thing.
Get me out!"
    The porter stood watching him and didn't move.
    "Jesus," Hazel said, "Jesus."
    The porter didn't move. "Jesus been a long time gone,"
he said in a sour triumphant voice.

But the net result of these differences between O'Connor's earliest fiction and *Wise Blood* is probably by this
time more than clear. On the artistic level, first of all, she
was certainly seeking in her first novel a means of lifting
her material out of a kind of lowly realism. She wanted to
wrench this early material into something much stranger
and more intense, much more startling and provocative.
As we have seen, she went, in a sense, too far in this direction in *Wise Blood*—the cartoon-like figures of Enoch
Emery and the Hawkses do not really appear again after-
ward; and in the second novel *The Violent Bear It Away*
we see her in retreat from the extreme tactics of *Wise
Blood*.
    It is certainly clear that some time before the onslaught
of her illness, O'Connor had begun to find the friendly
stance she had adopted toward the reader in her earliest
work an encumbrance and—one suspects—an evasion, for
it had already been drastically altered in the early drafts
of *Wise Blood*. One does not know what in her private life
helps to account for the fact that this writer who began
so normally was to adopt so fierce and forbidding a mode
of fiction in all her subsequent work, but in any case there
is in the early pieces nothing importunate, accusatory, or
prophetic, even in the story out of which came the very
strange *Wise Blood*—the heavily evangelistic and often
rigidly doctrinaire strain of her later books is barely

visible here at all. The early pieces present a picture of an author quite at peace with the world, it seems to me, and perhaps this picture had to be altered simply because it had been false from the beginning. It may be a factor that it was during this early period that Miss O'Connor first left the South, her Catholic family and conservative hometown. Perhaps her deepening sense of how nearly alone she was, among American artists and intellectuals, in her strict commitment to a Christian view of life helped to drive her to the hostile and prophetic mode of her first novel. Her experiences at Iowa and her reading during these years—of West's *Miss Lonelyhearts,* for instance—may of course have played their parts as well.

It goes almost without saying that in matters of sheer craft her skill enormously increased; one need only compare the first story "The Geranium" to the brilliant late story "Judgement Day." The success of "Judgement Day" may be partly explained by the fact that, being a rewriting of the early "The Geranium," it landed, so to speak, in tonal territory somewhere between the mild and warm early period and the much harsher later period. Actually, there is an unpublished middle version of this tale, much closer to "The Geranium" than to "Judgement Day," which is included in the O'Connor papers at the Georgia College library in Milledgeville. This version went unpublished because it was thought—by someone—to be too much like "The Geranium." In June, 1955, O'Connor wrote her agent Elizabeth McKee that she planned to give the story a shot of ACTH, the steroid she was taking, and put it back in circulation—but she may not have worked on the tale again until she rewrote it as "Judgement Day" much later on. The basic attitude toward the old man is not much changed in the later story, but the texture of the piece is much more shrewdly done. The brilliant and crucial scenes between Dudley and the Negro Coleman at the mill and between Dudley and the Negro landowner at

Dudley's shack were composed for "Judgement Day," and they help to effect a dramatic balance between comic contempt for the old man and pity for him that is a high achievement indeed.

Chapter III

# The Violent Bear It Away

Flannery O'Connor seems to have sought, all her writing life, a means of approach to an audience whose religious sense she believed to be stunted and deformed, if not yet wholly defunct. The mocking, malevolent assault on the godless life that we get in *Wise Blood* gives way in her second novel, *The Violent Bear It Away*, to a much more focused attempt to convey, in more realistic and persuasive terms, the anguish and beauty of true religious experience. This is not to say that the problem of assent to O'Connor's odd and narrow view of life is absent in *The Violent Bear It Away*; there are certainly parts of the book where the tonal and philosophical barriers tend, once again, to set us against her. I suggested earlier that O'Connor would prove in the long run a difficult writer to assess—and clearly *The Violent Bear It Away* is not one of the easier books in the O'Connor canon to come to terms with. Rather serious problems arise, as we shall see, in the latter half of the book, and yet what is good in this novel is very good indeed; one can say that on the whole it is a book into whose general tone and spirit a reader can enter with considerable sympathy and pleasure.

The great strength of the book is its long opening section on the life of old Tarwater and his young nephew in the backwoods clearing called Powderhead, as remembered by the boy on the day of the uncle's death. In the sheer energy and conviction of its evocation of scene and character—of the ferocious old Tarwater, for instance, wildly prophesying to his sullen, disdainful nephew in the dirt yard of the clearing—this passage can stand beside almost anything in our recent literature. Indeed much of the appeal of the Powderhead story (which can be rather clearly separated from the rest of the novel, most of which takes place in the city, where the boy goes after his uncle's death) lies in the warmth and depth of its folk humor, a humor strongly reminiscent of the country humor of Faulkner—even Faulkner at his best—and farther back of Mark Twain.

It is not surprising to find that this section of the novel was written during the period of O'Connor's career which now stands out clearly as her most productive. One tends to link the Powderhead story with the final scene of *Wise Blood,* mainly because of the peculiarly satisfying tonal balance between the comedy of everyday human conflict, on the one hand, and high religious seriousness, on the other, that they both achieve—and in fact the two passages are not far apart in their dates of composition. The opening of *The Violent Bear It Away* was among the earliest pieces O'Connor wrote after she had recovered from the first attack of her disease and seen *Wise Blood* through the press. She often remarked, in later years, that *The Violent Bear It Away* took her seven years to write (it appeared in 1960) ; and indeed Fitzgerald remembers seeing a version of the Powderhead story in 1953. It was probably this early version that was published, as a chapter of a novel-in-progress, in 1955 in *New World Writing* under the title "You Can't Be Any Poorer than Dead." [1] Between 1953 and 1956 O'Connor published, besides this opening of a new novel, no fewer than ten short stories, including many of her best. "The Life You Save May Be Your Own," for instance, is of this

1. Flannery O'Connor, "You Can't Be Any Poorer than Dead," *New World Writing,* VIII (October, 1955), 81–97. Reprinted in *The Complete Stories.*

period, as well as "The River," "A Circle in the Fire," "A Temple of the Holy Ghost," and "Good Country People"—all of which appeared first in periodicals such as the *Kenyon Review* and *Sewanee Review* and then in the 1955 collection *A Good Man Is Hard to Find*.

These were good years for O'Connor in more ways than one—good years not only in terms of fine work abundantly produced, but also, because these works were finding easy entry into respected magazines and then in collections and were winning national prizes (three O. Henry awards, for instance, in this period), good years in terms of greatly increased visibility in the literary world. *A Good Man Is Hard to Find* was much more widely and attentively reviewed than *Wise Blood*; Caroline Gordon wrote a serious and respectful review of it for the New York *Times,* and the New York *Herald Tribune* featured on its front page a quite perceptive review by Sylvia Stallings titled "Flannery O'Connor: A New Shining Talent Among Our Storytellers." [2] In many places, of course, there was still deep confusion as to what exactly this strange writer was about—a confusion stemming mainly from continued failure to understand her deep-seated religiosity. William Esty seems to have summed up for a number of unenthusiastic readers a major complaint about O'Connor when he wrote of her "over-ingenuous horrifics" in a 1958 essay for *Commonweal* that achieved considerable notoriety.[3] Esty named one of his schools of modern fiction the "Paul Bowles-Flannery O'Connor Cult of Gratuitous Grotesque," a formulation blunt enough to be seized by O'Connor admirers as a convenient focal point for O'Connor apologia. Anyone who perceives O'Connor's true meaning, they argued,

2. Sylvia Stallings, "Flannery O'Connor: A New Shining Light Among Our Storytellers," *New York Herald Tribune Book Review,* June 5, 1955, p. 1.

3. William Esty, "In America, Intellectual Bomb Shelters," *Commonweal,* LXVII (March 7, 1958), 586–88.

will see that almost nothing in her work is gratuitous, least of all her use of the grotesque.

With the publication of *The Violent Bear It Away*, the chain of reviews lengthened again, but with much the same kind of mixed response as after *A Good Man Is Hard to Find*. There was still abundant confusion as to O'Connor's fundamental aims. A number of readers seemed hardly even to suspect that old Tarwater was drawn as a sympathetic figure, and they therefore tended to view Rayber, not the boy, as the protagonist. The *New Statesman*, for instance, stated that the main part of the book "concerns the struggles of the schoolmaster first to help the boy to escape the obsessional madness of the old man and then to save himself and his son from the boy." [4] The *Times Literary Supplement*, even while being moved by O'Connor's "extraordinary power and virtuosity," saw the book in much the same way; the true subject, its reviewer felt, was Rayber's problem in coping with his idiot son and with his "spiritually-warped" nephew.[5]

And of course one can easily see why the tendency—even, to some extent, the need—of modern readers would be to identify with the "emancipated" Rayber and not with the fanatical old man. On its face, Rayber's story seems to be one of the classic, now almost mythic growing-up stories of the modern age: the story of the sensitive youth who repudiates, usually with considerable emotional anguish, what he considers to be the old-fashioned religious illusion, piety, and prejudice of his family and hometown congregation and grows up into freedom and knowledge and commitment of a very different sort. An almost pure example of this story in fiction is James Baldwin's *Go Tell It on the Mountain* (a book

4. Gerda Charles, review of *The Violent Bear It Away*, in *New Statesman*, LX (September 24, 1960), 445–46.

5. Anonymous review of *The Violent Bear It Away*, in *Times Literary Supplement*, October 14, 1960, p. 666.

which appeared the same year as another, but very contrary novel of education, O'Connor's *Wise Blood*).

But in any case the story told in *The Violent Bear It Away* is, for many readers of serious novels, a story which is, in effect, very close to their own. It is easy for us to see it as our own story but told in reverse—that is, with the moral that we ourselves tend to attach to it foiled at every turn, through the mockery of Rayber's scientific humanism and through the lyric celebration of Tarwater's yielding, at the end, to the vision of the old man. In this book, in other words, we see, once we begin to examine it closely, that to grow away from the seeming innocence and illusion of literalistic religious belief is made to seem wrong and tragic, and to cling to it or to revert to it, in contempt of the modern intellectual world, is made to seem good and right. Insofar as the novel has a thesis, this is certainly it, and of course the thesis—and in fact the narrative pattern itself—is exactly the same as in *Wise Blood*. But in *The Violent Bear It Away*, as I have already suggested, the thesis does not override and overwhelm the action of the story nearly so roughly as it does in *Wise Blood*; in most of the book, certainly in the Powderhead story at the beginning, the author's presence is much less oppressively felt—partly because the story unfolds mainly from the point of view of the boy himself, so that we need not constantly accede to the fact that he sees justly, but just that he sees oddly, he sees differently, simply that, in effect, he sees as he does.

One need hardly repeat that to write in a plausible and moving way about religious belief is difficult today for any writer—but especially difficult in America, where there has never been a real tradition of serious religious literature, much less a general "revival" of religious writing as there has been in France. Of course even there the loneliness and isolation of the Christian artist can be keenly felt, as we noted in the passage from Bernanos in which he visits on his heathen readers his prophetic anger and contempt. Even in an earlier time Paul Claudel, for all his success and acclaim, could also be overcome from time to time with a sense of his oddness and alienation. He wrote, for instance, to Gide from Tientsin in 1908:

> You must understand the position of a Catholic, in this happy epoch of ours, when all the books, papers, reviews that he receives from France, bring him bundles and cart-loads of nothing but insults, mockery, attacks of every sort and from every side upon all that he reveres in the world, and news of ruin, persecution and apostasy. For me, if any-one attacks the Church, it is as if he had struck my father or my mother. . . . For you Christ is no more than any other figure from History or Legend. But for me he is something quite other.[6]

Similarly, O'Connor wrote once to a friend that she thought novels should be about matters of the gravest concern and that for her "this is always the conflict between an attraction for the Holy and the disbelief in it that we breathe in with the air of the times." [7] And from O'Connor we also have this oft-quoted statement on the Christian writer's need of a special means of approach to an audience hostile to his view of the world: "When you can assume that your audience holds the same beliefs you do, you can relax a little and use more normal ways of talking to it; when you have to assume that it does not, then you have to make your vision apparent by shock—to the hard of hearing you shout, and for the almost blind you draw large and startling figures." [8]

Such lines—along with the typically bitter, contemp-

6. *The Correspondence Between Paul Claudel and André Gide*, trans. John Russell, with introduction and notes by Robert Mallet (New York, 1952), 70.

7. In a letter apparently written to John Hawkes, who cites this passage in "Flannery O'Connor's Devil," *Sewanee Review*, LXX (Summer, 1962), 397.

8. Flannery O'Connor, "The Fiction Writer and His Country," in *The Living Novel: A Symposium*, ed. Granville Hicks (New York, 1957), 157–64. Available now in *Mystery and Manners*, ed. Sally and Robert Fitzgerald

tuous, morose, sometimes furious tone of contemporary Christian writing itself—remind us that our century may well be witnessing the death-throes of Christian art. This sentence of T. S. Eliot's in which he warns Christians (in the 1935 essay "Religion and Literature") to beware the seductions of anti-Christian literature sounds a sombre and painful note indeed: "What I do wish to affirm is that the whole of modern literature is corrupted by what I call Secularism, that it is simply unaware of, simply cannot understand the meaning of, the primacy of the supernatural over the natural life: of something which I assume to be our primary concern." [9] And of course the primary concern of modern readers is not for further adventure into the mystery of God's will for men, into the mystery and agony of the attainment of true belief and holiness—but for the mystery and agony of life *without* belief, of life which must somehow be lived without the hope of finding final truth at all. And the characters that strike most deeply into the modern consciousness are ones who appear to us as delicately drawn images of our own uncertainty, wonderment, and confusion—an Ishmael, a Quentin Compson, a Joe Christmas, Brett and Jake and the other lost children of Hemingway's sundered world; in more recent times, even a Yossarian, for whom all life has come to seem like absurd comedy; a Jacob Horner, whose first line to the reader—I am, I think, Jacob Horner—perfectly captures ourselves in a certain mood, a mood in which everything looks uncertain and unreal and we feel ourselves caught in a constant crisis of doubt and indecision, of inability to find any grounds on which to base a human act or decision.

But all of this is only, perhaps, to repeat that in the context of modern American literature, O'Connor presents the initial problem—the bafflement of her reviewers

9. Eliot, "Religion and Literature," *Selected Essays.*

through the years bears this out, I think—of the unaccustomed feel of a writer strangely, almost unbelieveably, unattuned to the ambiguities, uncertainties, bafflements of life and thought as most of us know and experience them every day. Here was a writer attuned, rather, to the old ways where life rested ultimately on the all-embracing certainty of *the answer:* I am the way, the truth, and the life; a writer for whom this answer looms, sometimes suffocatingly close to the immediate action of her stories, sometimes more artfully distanced, over everything she writes—the same answer returned to again and again, the same answer always blocking the path of inquiry and exploration; a writer who could serenely say that as a Christian writer she was blessed "with the prophetic vision that is good for all time," who could say, "I see by the light of Christian orthodoxy and what I see in the world I see in relation to that";[10] a writer who renounced everything in which the modern heretical world has attempted to find solace. A fellow southerner, Katherine Anne Porter, wrote of yet another woman writer, this one English, a paragraph that stands as a sharp reminder of the kind of artist that has come to seem quintessentially modern in her vision of life, and from which the fixed doctrine of the O'Connor fiction is so many worlds apart:

> She was full of secular intelligence primed with the profane virtues, with her love not only of the world of all the arts created by the human imagination, but a love of life itself and of daily living, a spirit at once gay and severe, exacting and generous, a born artist and a sober craftsman; and she had no plan whatever for her personal salvation; or the personal salvation even of someone else; brought no doctrine; no dogma. Life, the life of this world, here and now, was a great mystery, no one could fathom it; and death was the end.[11]

10. O'Connor, "The Fiction Writer and His Country," 162.
11. Katherine Anne Porter, *The Collected Essays* (New York, 1970), 71. To Porter's statement about Virginia Woolf, a Christian

This is Virginia Woolf. But if the evangelical confidence and fervor of O'Connor is far removed from the likes of Woolf, it is, on the other hand, not so removed from the work of another writer of Woolf's time, D. H. Lawrence —for Lawrence had a plan of salvation too. Yet of course Lawrence's prophecy—though like O'Connor's it sometimes seemed simplistic and unreasonable to the point of absurdity—expressed feelings common to many people disturbed by our modern obeisance to science and technology. O'Connor's prophecy, on the other hand, is hardly more fresh or modern—and I think she would have enjoyed the irony that follows herself—than what one gets in religious tracts handed one on street corners, than the tracts the street preacher Hawks might have handed round in *Wise Blood*. Is this not, for instance, a rather fair summation of O'Connor's religious thought?

> Today only a small minority of earth's population appreciate the name JEHOVAH and worship the God who bears it. The vast majority have put God out of mind, or at best offer only token worship. Giving free rein to their own passions and being engrossed with selfish goals, they no longer care to keep in mind a God who stands for truth, love and righteousness. They have substituted their own puerile

---

reader might reply that though Woolf did indeed find much to celebrate in human society and in ordinary human endeavors and relationships, the failure of human society of her time was also what drove her to despair and suicide.

Regarding the contrasting negativism of modern Christian novelists, an interesting statement about the French Catholic writer Mauriac appears in Martin Turnell's essay on this writer in his *The Art of French Fiction* (London, 1959), 359:

> What is disconcerting about Mauriac's religion is that it is a religion of negation. No contemporary writer excels him in the vigour of his onslaught on the complacent middle classes or the frequency with which he hits the target, but there is a gap between the Christian and the writer. The writer fails to give concrete embodiment to the positive qualities which religion should supply or to offer a positive standard at all. It seems, indeed, that the positive qualities are dissolved in the struggle with the Jansenist virus. That is why we are left with nothing but the improbable conversions and why he 'makes a mess' of his virtuous characters.

fancies, gods that fit in with their own human ideas, use-less gods that manifest the same imperfect characteristics as those of their makers.

Even the so-called wise men of this generation, theo-logians, philosophers, psychologists, scientists, consider the pure truth of God's holy Book, the Bible, to be beneath them, too childish to believe, its moral standard too circum-scribing to their aims and conduct. Instead, they worship themselves. They think of man as the great inventor, the civilizer, the one through whom all future progress and blessings must come. The nations have indeed forgotten God.

These paragraphs are from a 1970 issue of *The Watch-tower*, distributed by Jehovah's Witnesses; they form the opening of an article titled "Jehovah's Name to be De-clared in all the Earth." One may note in passing that there is also an article in this issue on Christian free will which goes, indirectly of course, as far toward explicat-ing the problem of free will in *The Violent Bear It Away* —is Tarwater really free to choose the devil or God?—as anything one sees in our critical journals. The Witnesses' strict distinction between things of the world and things of the spirit was doubtless pleasing to O'Connor; a line from a prominent Witness devotional writer, "No worldly ambitions can find any place in the highway of holiness," [12] could be set as epigraph over many an O'Connor story. Of course O'Connor could also make fine comedy out of the curious tenets and taboos of fundamentalist sects— the Witnesses' prohibition against the worship of visual images is crucial for instance, to the plot of her last story, "Parker's Back."

In any case, reviewers who grasped in the beginning what O'Connor was saying, who saw that her religious ideas were essentially the same as those of her fanatical heroes (she said herself, after all, of old Tarwater: "[He] is the hero of *The Violent Bear It Away,* and I'm right

12. Alda B. Harrison in *Jehovah's Witnesses,* ed. Marley Cole (New York, 1955), 63.

behind him 100 per cent" [13]) were often quite scandalized. Orville Prescott, reviewing the book in the New York *Times*, said that both Tarwaters were mad, simply mad, and therefore "hardly . . . adequate representatives of Christian faith, if that is what Miss O'Connor means them to be"—but in Prescott's mind it would seem that anyone who thinks he has a prophetic destiny to accept or not accept is mad by definition.[14] Arthur Mizener's reaction to the book in the *Sewanee Review* is somewhat more interesting:

> The charitable view . . . must be that the election of such people [as the Tarwaters] dramatizes the fact that salvation is by grace alone and that the ignorant, like children around whom the prison walls have not yet closed, receive the divine election more easily than the knowing. But when we are asked to take Tarwater and his great-uncle this way, some of us benighted folk, anyhow, are likely to feel an unexpected sympathy with the doctrine of infant damnation: we are told that they are saved, but all we are shown is their savage ignorance. . . . there is . . . something disturbing about the savagely ignorant man's incongruous collection of ill-defined dogmas, however "sincere" his faith. Whatever the shortcomings of reason, there is a kind of fideism in denying its relevance so completely as this.[15]

Here, in other words, is a reader for whom the *données* of the book proved, at least in this early reading of it, too formidable—and there are points in the book where, even today, the honest reader will probably admit to a sneaking sympathy with Mizener's position. Yet the book has survived such criticism as that—and there was a great deal of it. A decade of accommodating ourselves, as it were, to O'Connor's persistently strange and narrow view of things is what has made it possible, perhaps, for us

13. Granville Hicks, "A Writer at Home with Her Heritage," *Saturday Review*, XLV (May 12, 1962), 22–23.

14. Orville Prescott, review of *The Violent Bear It Away*, in New York *Times*, February 24, 1960, p. 35.

15. Arthur Mizener, review of *The Violent Bear It Away*, in *Sewanee Review*, LXIX (Winter, 1961), 161–63.

to read her today with greater appreciation—to enjoy, for instance, in a more relaxed way the delicate tonality of the Powderhead story that opens the book. O'Connor seems to have survived the early hypercritical stage of reaction to her work and to have crossed over—even somewhat prematurely, like many contemporary writers —into the stage of scholarly explication and exegesis. But her work is still young enough that the truly critical questions remain the most interesting ones to ask.

## 2

Although the narrative method that O'Connor uses in Part One of *The Violent Bear It Away* was one that she made little use of in other writings, she employs it here to consummate advantage. Her short stories have given her the reputation of a writer whose special forte was her architectonic ability; the characteristic O'Connor short story is a squarely rigged, tightly plotted piece unfolding a series of neatly arranged events very scrupulously paced, with quite sparing use of the free-flowing, dreamlike memory passages (on the part of the characters) which in most modern fiction are so familiar. Her work tends, in other words, to be largely foreground with much of the meaning embodied in delicately contoured conversations among the main characters, sometimes in a few rapid exchanges, and in the sharp impact on the protagonist of a series of external events—often forming a gradually escalating assault on his sense of worldly power and accomplishment—which the reader observes at firsthand. Her stories begin, more often than not, *in medias res*, and the background that she weaves in on the characters is scant and pointed; she likes to try to sum them up—it is a mark, of course, of her contempt for these usually irreligious individuals—in a few pithy lines or well-chosen anecdotes. (Consider her treatment, for instance, of the members of the vacationing family, even of the grandmother, in "A Good Man Is Hard to Find.")

These are particularly fitting habits for the composition of short stories (though today, of course, many good stories make use of much more fluid and expansive forms), but what is somewhat stranger is that these strict habits held sway in O'Connor's first novel as well. She seemed to aim for an almost purely dramatic form, in which everything significant about the characters could be expressed in what they said and did in a given, rather strictly controlled situation, rather than in expansive exploration of their states of mind. Her comments to Fitzgerald about Eliot's *The Family Reunion* seem to bear this out. She maintained, Fitzgerald wrote, at the time she was writing *Wise Blood*, that Eliot's Harry "actually had pushed his wife overboard, against a theory that he had done so only in his mind." She said, "If nothing happened, there's no story." [16]

But the Powderhead story of *The Violent Bear It Away* (Part One, that is, of this three-part novel) is a thoroughgoing piece of what is often called stream-of-consciousness writing; the boy's stream of thought is the real subject of the story, and his past life is revealed through the memories which flow in and out of his mind as he tries to decide, on the day of his uncle's death, what to do with the rest of his life. And it seems to me that nothing would have served better than this device to focus the drama where it should be here: on the boy's struggle with the question of whether to follow the fiercely religious—half-crazy, as it seems to him at times—ways of the old man or to forsake his ways and take his normal place in the great world outside, "to begin to make his own acquaintance," as the boy puts it in one place. By using the boy's state of acute emotional conflict and indecision after his uncle's death as a frame to hold the telling of the history of their lives together at Powderhead, O'Connor keeps this imminent and inescapable

16. Fitzgerald's introduction to *Everything That Rises Must Converge.*

decision of the boy before the reader in high relief all through this section of the book. And at the same time the drama of the wonderfully comical but oddly fetching, in many ways idyllic, life of the old man and the boy together in the woods is, of course, intensified for having such a frame, for being recreated in the boy's mind at so tense and critical a time.

Part One contains, in actual time, only the hours elapsing between the death of old Tarwater at the breakfast table and the arrival of Tarwater late that night at the door of Rayber, his younger uncle who lives in the city. Very little happens in the foreground in terms of extended action in the usual sense, although those few things are major events in the boy's life. We learn about the first one in the rolling opening sentence of the book: "Francis Marion Tarwater's uncle had been dead for only half a day when the boy got too drunk to finish digging his grave and a Negro named Buford Munson, who had come to get a jug filled, had to finish it and drag the body from the breakfast table where it was still sitting and bury it in a decent and Christian way, with the sign of its Savior at the head of the grave and enough dirt on top to keep the dogs from digging it up." The foreground action is completed near the end of the section, where a night-bird wakens Tarwater from his drunken sleep; not knowing that his Negro neighbor has buried his great-uncle, he proceeds to burn the shack down, with the old man presumably still sitting at the breakfast table where he died, and to fly out of the woods onto a highway where he hitches a ride to the city.

The rest of the Powderhead story—nearly all of it, that is—shows Tarwater, during the hours after his uncle's death, thinking back over and trying to reinterpret in the light of his new independence the crucial scenes of his life under the old man's extraordinary tutelage. And what evolves, in brilliantly lifelike dimension, is a kaleiodoscopic succession of highly animated scenes and images and dialogues, with the ferocious old man as central character and the boy as sullen, though always alert, witness —the author very nearly silent and invisible.

As the boy tries, fitfully, to dig the grave, gets drunk on old Tarwater's forbidden moonshine, finally sets fire to the house as his first major act of defiance, and hitches a ride to the city, he remembers, nevertheless, the old man's exhortation to "justify Christ's redemption," accept the mantle of prophecy, and baptize Rayber's idiot child. The problem is that Tarwater has never been sure even of the old man's truth, much less the nature of his own "call." We learn that old Tarwater has told him that if he himself had not gotten the child baptized by the time he died, it would be up to the boy. "It'll be the first mission the Lord sends you." But the boy had doubted all along that his first mission would be to baptize a dim-witted child. He had said, "Oh no, it won't be. . . . He don't mean for me to finish up your leavings."

As Tarwater dawdles on the back steps of the shack, listens in vain for some sign of his election, and feebly plies the earth where his uncle wanted to be laid, he struggles to reckon his own position in regard to his uncle's doctrine. And through the boy's reflections on their life together we see the old man in a series of vividly contrasting moods: stern and commanding, penitent and self-debasing, fired up with a blistering rage, querulous and argumentative, and constantly smitten with desire to tell and retell the critical episodes of his lifelong war against his godless relatives—in effect, the whole hostile, godless, unregenerate world outside Powderhead. These relatives consist, mainly, of old Tarwater's sister and her two children, a daughter who died giving birth to Tarwater in a wreck, and a son, Rayber, who adopted the baby and then had it stolen from him by the old man when it was only a few months old. Tarwater has heard the stories many times, and he listens with varying degrees of interest, feeling sometimes contempt for the old man and sometimes awe and love—at times simply boredom. Sometimes the old man reenacts the scenes he tells just as they originally happened, as in the story of the time his sister "worked a perify on him" and got him sent to the asylum by having spies stationed behind her door when the old man came to harangue her. And how the old man carries on! He jumps up and starts shouting and prophesying there in the clearing—with no one to hear but the boy—just as he had done at his sister's: "Ignore the Lord Jesus, as long as you can! Spit out the bread of life and sicken on honey. . . . The Lord is preparing a prophet with fire in his hand and eye and the prophet is moving toward the city with his warning." And note this deft description of the boy's response:

> He might have been shouting to the silent woods that encircled them. While he was in his frenzy, the boy would take up the shotgun and hold it to his eye and sight along the barrel, but sometimes as his uncle grew more and more wild, he would lift his face from the gun for a moment with a look of uneasy alertness, as if while he had been inattentive, the old man's words had been dropping one by one into him and now, silent, hidden in his bloodstream, were moving steadily toward some goal of their own.

To this image of the boy coolly sighting along the gunbarrel as the old man prophesies there in the clearing and the chickens scratch in the dirt of the yard, one could add many more images just as sharp: the image, for instance, of the old man lying in his homemade coffin on the back porch "with his stomach rising over the top like overleavened bread," saying "This is the end of us all"; the image of the "red sweating bitten face" of the comically humorless and ineffectual Rayber "bobbing up and down through the corn," with the pink flowered hat of the welfare lady he was to marry appearing behind as the two of them make their futile trip to the shack through the old man's corn field to try to rescue the boy (a crossing suggestively reappearing, as made by one or another

of the characters, in a number of episodes of the story) ;
the image of the old man sitting dead as a doornail, up-
right at the breakfast table, with the boy across from
him simply finishing his breakfast "in a kind of sullen
embarrassment"; the image of the drunken Tarwater
falling asleep, late that afternoon, in the sandy cove
where the old man kept his supply of moonshine, the black
jug dripping sun-colored drops of liquor onto his dirty
overalls; the image of him later that evening, crawling
over the littered ground under the moonlit shack setting
the small fires that will consume the house as he flees.

Many of the stark pictures that the reader's memory
continues to call up—and O'Connor's deft pictorial ability
serves her in this tale, it seems to me, as well as it did
in anything she wrote—are images from scenes or episodes
of the story that have such distinct shapes of their own as
to impel one to separate them from the stream of the narrative as almost self-contained vignettes. As one thumbs
through the book, looking over these brief vignettes, one
realizes that nearly all of them are funny, are built on
some inherently comic situation; yet tonally they are a
far cry from the generally barren farce of *Wise Blood*
(always excepting the final scene of that book telling
Hazel's repentance and death), for here the comedy rests
firmly on highly compelling—and unquestionably O'Connor's most warmly conceived—characterizations. Indeed
in the Powderhead story interest in character is clearly
much more dominant than is generally the case in O'Connor. As in most fine narrative literature, it is as if the
writer were indulging the reader in the peculiarly satisfying fictive illusion—an illusion that is usually endan-
gered by highly ideological writing—that it is the characters who, once put in motion, wield and manipulate the
writer, rather than vice versa, that their lives demand to
be honestly and fully told whether or not any deeper
purpose of the author is served.

In this opening section of the book the reader's attitude

toward the characters is deftly shaped from the opening
lines of the story, and the reader can easily adopt, it
seems to me, the attitude of affectionate and amused
tolerance of this pair's queerness and comical absurdity
that the story is attempting to inspire. (The more disturbing part of the book, as we shall see, is liable to be
the latter half, as the story begins much more plainly to
move toward sanction and celebration of the old man's
religious vision.) What is particularly satisfying about
the Powderhead section is that this passage constantly
teeters on the edge of outrageous comedy, that is of
farce, but, much like Faulkner's *As I Lay Dying*, never
quite tips over into it. Farcical elements are certainly
there—the old man's crazy antics, of course, for one
thing; the boy's occasionally monstrous, however sly,
vindictiveness (he decides to dig the old man's grave
under the fig tree because he would be good for the figs);
and many broadly comic details of Powderhead life and
manners. But the tonal control is firm enough that the
distance between reader and characters can also swiftly
close, as in the scene in which Tarwater, running away
in the night from the burning shack, seems to see the old
man's eyes staring from the flames: ". . . he glanced
over his shoulder and saw that the pink moon had dropped
through the roof of the shack and was bursting and he
began to run, forced on through the woods by two bulg-
ing silver eyes that grew in immense astonishment in
the center of the fire behind him"; or in the sudden sharp
descriptions of the boy's painful secret predicament: "In
the darkest, most private part of his soul, hanging up-
side-down like a sleeping bat, was the certain, undeniable
knowledge that he was not hungry for the bread of life."
Such moments are given to the old man as well; here he
is telling of taking the shotgun to his nephew Rayber
when he had come to rescue the infant Tarwater:

> The second shot flushed the righteousness of his [Rayber's]
> face and left it blank and white, revealing that there was

nothing underneath it, revealing, the old man sometimes admitted, his own failure as well, for he had tried and failed, long ago, to rescue the nephew. He had kidnapped him when the child was seven and had taken him to the backwoods and baptized him and instructed him in the facts of his Redemption, but the instruction had lasted only for a few years; in time the child had set himself a different course. There were moments when the thought that he might have helped the nephew on to his new course himself became so heavy in the old man that he would stop telling the story to Tarwater, stop and stare in front of him as if he were looking into a pit which had opened up before his feet.

Such a passage as this shows old Tarwater in a very human light—regardless, of course, of how one might feel about the significance of those "facts of redemption" that had failed to transform the boy Rayber for all time.

Of course the fact that the old man's behavior is presented in this early section through the eyes of the doubting Tarwater makes it possible for the author to give full play to a critical, rather objective view of him. (Rayber's much harsher rejection in Parts Two and Three is generally meant to ring much more clearly false.) The tonal subtlety of the Powderhead section is well illustrated by a passage on the second page of the story. "The old man," we learn, "who said he was a prophet, had raised the boy to expect the Lord's call himself and to be prepared for the day he would hear it." "Who said he was a prophet"—this claim of the old man is put forward, in effect, by the boy, merely for what it is worth; and that, in a sense, is the tenor of the whole Powderhead story. There is a remarkable paragraph in this passage in which we see O'Connor expertly handling an episode that is almost a convention of religious narrative, the lesson in humility in which the Christian hero —or martyr in the making, one thinks in particular of Eliot's Thomas in *Murder in the Cathedral*—learns not to overestimate his own righteousness or the value of his own mission:

He had been called in his early youth and had set out for
the city to proclaim the destruction awaiting a world that
had abandoned its Savior. He proclaimed from the midst of
his fury that the world would see the sun burst in blood
and fire and while he raged and waited, it rose every morning, calm and contained in itself, as if not only the world,
but the Lord Himself had failed to hear the prophet's message. It rose and set, rose and set on a world that turned
from green to white and green to white and green to white
again. It rose and set and he despaired of the Lord's listening. Then one morning he saw to his joy a finger of fire
coming out of it and before he could turn, before he could
shout, the finger had touched him and the destruction he
had been waiting for had fallen in his own brain and his
own body. His blood had been burned dry and not the blood
of the world.

Or so the old man believed. This is a cunningly composed
passage indeed. The language is, of course, not the old
man's, but it reflects it in its preacher-like repetitions
("rose and set, rose and set . . .") and in the biblical
wording the old man used so vigorously. "Judgement may
rack your bones," he would tell Tarwater when the boy
challenged him, or "Listen boy . . . even the mercy of
the Lord burns." But more than anything else, it is
probably the rhythm of this paragraph—the sustained
build towards the final line—that renders it so effective;
this is so in spite of the fact that the final image, of the
finger of fire touching the old man himself, is, unlike most
of the highly particularized writing of this section, mysterious and mystical and unexplained in terms of what
literally happened.

It is not necessary to go from scene to scene, pointing
the approving finger at this or that special felicity, but
one might draw out two other episodes—or vignettes—in
which the delicately toned comedy of this peculiar relationship is especially satisfying. One episode in which
the volatile temper of the old man is wonderfully played
against the tight-lipped, often sullen and facetious temper of the child is the scene in which old Tarwater gives

the boy instructions for his burial. The old man could not be more serious about his burial plans, yet without demeaning him in the slightest, O'Connor fully exploits the comic angle. The old man has made his wooden box himself, inscribed it MASON TARWATER, WITH GOD, and lain down in it on the back steps, saying, as we have seen, "This is the end of us all." What follows is too long to quote in full—it runs about two pages—but at the heart of the scene is this vivid exchange which takes place as the boy, looking down at his uncle in the box, listens to the old man's directions for his proper Christian burial.

"It's too much of you for the box," Tarwater said. "I'll have to sit on the lid to press you down or wait until you rot a little."

"Don't wait," old Tarwater had said. "Listen. If it ain't feasible to use the box when the time comes, if you can't lift it or whatever, just get me in the hole but I want it deep. I want it ten foot, not just eight, ten. You can roll me to it if nothing else. I'll roll. Get two boards and set them down the steps and start me rolling and dig where I stop and don't let me roll over into it until it's deep enough. Prop me with some bricks so I won't roll into it and don't let the dogs nudge me over the edge before it's finished. You better pen up the dogs," he said.

"What if you die in bed?" the boy asked. "How'm I going to get you down the stairs?"

"I ain't going to die in bed," the old man said. "As soon as I hear the summons, I'm going to run downstairs. I'll get as close to the door as I can. If I should get stuck up there, you'll have to roll me down the stairs, that's all."

"My Lord," the child said.

The old man sat up in the box and brought his fist down on the edge of it. "Listen," he said. "I never asked much of you. I taken you and raised you and saved you from that ass in town and now all I'm asking in return is when I die to get me in the ground where the dead belong and set up a cross over me to show I'm there. That's all in the world I'm asking you to do. I ain't ever asking you to go for the niggers and try to get me in the plot with my daddy. I could ask you that but I ain't. I'm doing everything to make it

easy for you. All I'm asking you is to get me in the ground
and set up a cross."

"I'll be doing good if I get you in the ground," Tarwater
said. "I'll be too wore out to set up any cross. I ain't bothering with trifles."

"Trifles!" his uncle hissed. "You'll learn what a trifle is
on the day those crosses are gathered!"

The vigorous conviction with which such scenes as this are
written is likely to put to rest any forebodings the reader
may have about the motion of the story toward some religious thesis. In fact one is almost moved to complain that
if the author could write like this—that is, in so relaxed,
good-tempered, yet sharply concentrated a way—about
such characters as these, why did she do so so seldom?
Here she is writing about individuals who, living a life
in which religious questions are the only questions of
vital concern, have her respect and sympathy. But generally—in nearly all the short stories, for instance—she
chose to write about people who were not interested in
religious questions and for whose other, wordly concerns
she had no patience and not a great deal of understanding. But then Powderhead, the true religious community,
is in our time an anomaly, as no one knew better than
O'Connor; and one can easily imagine such a writer turning aside, perhaps with bitter regret and driven by her
evangelistic and also her simply belligerent instincts, to
the real world outside where the grossly uneven clash
between religious belief and godlessness had to be joined,
and where, unfortunately, in many ways, for her art,
the reader had to be seen as adversary, as one to be
brought over, to be shocked and frightened, if necessary,
into submission, or—in moods where she felt the hope-
lessness of making him see—at least punished with pain
and abuse. After the Powderhead idyll comes, by way of
Tarwater's attempt to adjust himself to the modern
world, the familiar O'Connor story of evil life in the city.

And what is curious is that though in the eyes of the world it is Powderhead life that is strange and almost exotically remote, it is this life that O'Connor makes most real and alluring, and that it is life in the normal world outside, in a teacher's brick bungalow on an average city street, that seems by contrast odd and nearly unreal.

One of the episodes in which the folk humor of the Powderhead story is at its most zestful is the scene in which the truant officer makes his way out to the clearing to try to make old Tarwater send the boy to school. The reader has the pleasure of being able to draw quite close to this odd pair and to enjoy with them their triumph against the gullible intruder. Even here, however, the comedy, for all its playfulness, touches bottom ground of a conflict that is basically serious; what we get is a vivid view of the old man and the boy standing together against the foolish and deluded world outside, and their sense of embattlement is symbolic of that of the whole community of true believers, who live, in a sense, under constant siege from the hostile and powerful secular world. The Tarwaters, in other words, are alone against all—and yet they have their joke on that all from time to time:

> The truant officer had come only once. The Lord had told the old man to expect it and what to do and old Tarwater had instructed the boy in his part against the day when, as the devil's emissary, the officer would appear. When the time came and they saw him cutting across the field, they were ready. The child got behind the house and the old man sat on the steps and waited. When the officer, a thin bald-headed man with red galluses, stepped out of the field onto the packed dirt of the yard, he greeted old Tarwater warily and commenced his business as if he had not come for it. He sat down on the steps and spoke of poor weather and poor health. Finally, gazing out over the field, he said, "You got a boy don't you, that ought to be in school?"
>
> "A fine boy," the old man said, "and I wouldn't stand in his way if anybody thought they could teach him. You boy!" he called. The boy didn't come at once. "Oh you boy!" the old man shouted.

In a few minutes Tarwater appeared from around the side of the house. His eyes were open but not well-focused. His head rolled uncontrollably on his slack shoulders and his tongue lolled in his open mouth.

"He ain't bright," the old man said, "but he's a mighty good boy. He knows to come when you call him."

"Yes," the truant officer said, "well yes, but it might be best to leave him in peace."

"I don't know, he might take to schooling," the old man said. "He ain't had a fit for going on two months."

"I speck he better stay at home," the officer said. "I wouldn't want to put a strain on him," and he commenced to speak of other things. Shortly he took his leave and the two of them watched with satisfaction as the diminishing figure moved back across the field and the red galluses were finally lost to view.

But we turn now to another feature of the presentation of Tarwater's *bellum intestinum* on the day of his uncle's death: the inner voice that begins speaking to him at the breakfast table where the uncle dies, helps him interpret his past life at Powderhead, argues with him about his present predicament, and finally presents the case for his repudiation of the old man. Everyone knows what it means, when faced with some important decision, to seem to carry on a mental argument with one's self and to be aware, in a sense, of voices arguing back and forth the pros and cons of this or that action. At first Tarwater clearly thinks of the voice that speaks to him after his uncle's death as simply his own voice grown aggressively strange and loud, but as he begins to answer the voice back, it comes to seem more and more as if the voice were separate and other. The voice assumes the role of the cynic out to make a mockery of Tarwater's religious pretensions and commences to preach on a theme that he will continue all through the boy's ordeal at Rayber's and his return to Powderhead at the end: if the old man was a true prophet and the boy destined to follow in his footsteps, where is the sign of his election?

You go ahead and put your feet in his shoes. Elisha after Elijah like he said. But jest lemme ast you this: where is the voice of the Lord? I haven't heard it. Who's called you this morning? Or any morning? Have you been told what to do? You ain't even heard the sound of natural thunder this morning. There ain't a cloud in the sky. The trouble with you, he concluded, is that you ain't got but just enough sense to believe every word he told you.

"The stranger," as the owner of the voice is often designated, makes fun of Tarwater's grave-digging efforts—what difference does it make anyway? he argues, and O'Connor gives him some amusing speeches parodying the heretic's literalistic arguments against Christian burial dogma. "Well now, the stranger said, don't you think any cross you set up in the year 1952 would be rotted out by the year the Day of Judgment comes in? . . . And lemme ast you this: what's God going to do with sailors drowned at sea that the fish have et and the fish that et them et by other fish and they et by yet others?" And what of those, he goes on, of whom there's nothing left to burn or bury?

If I burnt him, Tarwater said, it wouldn't be natural, it would be deliberate.

Oh I see, the stranger said. It ain't the Day of Judgment for him you're worried about. It's the Day of Judgment for you.

That's my bidnis, Tarwater said.

One reason that the use of these conversations between Tarwater and his inner voice—or between two aspects or sides of his own mind—is a fortunate device here in Part One is that it gives O'Connor a means of skirting Gordon's dictum of avoiding narration in the rural idiom of her primitive characters and allows her to make full use of her unusual gift for imitation of southern country speech and for capturing the essence of a character's thought and culture in his language. Hardly anything the narrator could say in her own language could quite match the stark immediacy and pointedness of these conversa-

tions Tarwater has with himself in his own idiom. Here
the voice is comparing the boy's plight with that of the
schoolteacher Rayber, who discovered that the old man
was a fraud:

> You see he was crazy all along, he continued. Wanted to
> make a prophet out of that schoolteacher too, but the school-
> teacher was too smart for him. He got away.
> He had somebody to come for him, Tarwater said. His
> daddy came and got him back. Nobody came and got me
> back.
> The schoolteacher himself come after you, the stranger
> said, and got shot in the leg and the ear for his trouble.
> I was not yet one year old, Tarwater said. A baby can't
> walk off and leave.
> You ain't a baby now, his friend said.
> The grave did not appear to get any deeper though he
> continued to dig. Look at the big prophet, the stranger
> jeered, and watched him from the shade of the speckled tree
> shadows. Lemme hear you prophesy something. The truth
> is the Lord ain't studying about you. You ain't entered His
> Head.

Thus this device is very cleverly and effectively used in
the Powderhead scenes of the book as a means of drama-
tizing the conflict of wills that Tarwater is suffering. But
to the extent that the boy comes to perceive this voice—
something which occurs mainly in the second half of the
novel—as not simply a part of himself but as somehow,
and this is not altogether clear, a being separate from
himself, one may feel that O'Connor pushes the device
too far. Even in the scenes at Powderhead, Tarwater begins to imagine a physical embodiment for the voice; he
seems to see him digging the grave alongside him at one
point and to envision him in "a broad-brimmed panama
hat." Still, the device is not psychologically implausible
as long as what we are really occupied with is simply a
process of Tarwater's mind, as long as we can see the
"stranger" as a feature of the boy's imagination. As C. S.
Lewis reminds us in *The Allegory of Love*, the religious
mind is particularly given to such mental allegories.

Lewis explains how it is that one who is aware of a divided will (as Tarwater is, so intensely) is naturally led to allegorize that conflict, to give form in his mind to the forces striving in him for mastery:

> To be thus conscious of the divided will is necessarily to turn the mind in upon itself. Whether it is the introspection which reveals the division, or whether the division, having first revealed itself in the experience of actual moral failure, provokes the introspection, need not here be decided. Whatever the causal order may be, it is plain that to fight against "Temptation" is also to explore the inner world; and it is scarcely less plain that to do so is to be already on the verge of allegory. We cannot speak, perhaps we can hardly think, of an "inner conflict" without a metaphor; and every metaphor is an allegory in little. . . . That unitary "soul" or "personality" which interests the [typical modern] novelist is for him [the religious writer occupied with the divided will] merely the arena in which the combatants meet: it is to the combatants . . . that he must attend. . . . It is idle to tell him that something with which he has been at death-grips for the last twenty-four hours is an "abstraction." [17]

While *The Violent Bear It Away* is certainly not itself an allegory, the existence in it of this extensively developed allegorized conflict—which grows more complicated later on as other allegorical elements are introduced— forms a link between this modern religious novel and the religious literature of the distant past.

This is all very well—but what becomes, as I have suggested, somewhat unsettling about the authorial use of this inner voice, this "stranger," later on in the novel is that O'Connor seems to be hypothesizing for it some kind of objective reality. Is it the devil himself Tarwater is contending with? Must we see, as Tarwater does, the stranger and the diabolic rapist of Part Three—who is certainly real, not a product of Tarwater's imagination

17. C. S. Lewis, *The Allegory of Love* (New York, 1958).

—as one and the same? But these hard questions may for the moment be put aside.

## 3

The great strength of *The Violent Bear It Away*, as already suggested, is the Powderhead story of Part One; the latter part of the book, which tells of Tarwater's anguished week with his atheistical uncle and his return to Powderhead as the murderer of the retarded child, is clearly a falling off. One might judge, from the amount of scholarly comment that is piling up about it, that it is this latter part of the book which is the most interesting and impressive. But one reason it has been the target of as much technical explanation as it has is that it is full of the kind of symbolic elements (O'Connor writers usually call them "images," but they are more fundamental than that) that present to the critic a ready chore of decoding and deciphering. The struggle in Tarwater's mind between his prideful, independent self and the side of him that continues to be pulled toward the old man becomes nearly the whole subject here; and it is generally described in an extremely abstract and mystical way— considerably less vivid and interesting than in Part One, where it was presented mainly in terms of the boy's conflicts with the amazing old Tarwater.

Two other forces emerge to give battle to "the stranger" for possession of Tarwater's mind and soul. One is described as "the silence," or "the silent country," which Tarwater is in constant danger of entering, which sometimes seems to surround him or to block his path, which seems at other times to be a silent eye watching him, and is, for instance, reflected in the eyes of the child Bishop; the other one is Tarwater's mysterious hunger, which will not be appeased by Rayber's city food, nor indeed—at this tortured time in the boy's life—by any mortal nourishment. Tarwater says, "It's like being empty is a thing in my stomach and it don't allow nothing else to come down in here." As the reader knows all along, and Tarwater comes to recognize at the end, his hunger is really for the bread of life—that is, for a return to life in Christ—and nothing else is ever going to satisfy him. This mysterious sense of an awesome silence all around him and of an unfathomable hunger that will not be satisfied are signs of the futility of his attempt to escape Jesus into the world, and they are really one and the same, as the following lines, I think, make clear: "Since the breakfast he had finished sitting in the presence of his uncle's corpse, he had not been satisfied by food, and his hunger had become like an insistent silent force inside him, a silence inside akin to the silence outside, as if the grand trap left him barely an inch to move in, barely an inch in which to keep himself inviolate." But the fact is, I'm afraid, that these antagonists—this silence and the boy's own hunger—are not very exciting ones; as adversaries they are not even as interesting as "the friendly stranger," who at least has a voice and continues to use it to mock Tarwater's vulnerability to these forces on the other side. The voice tells him, for instance, that his hunger is not a sign of election or of anything else—that what he has is probably just a case of worms!

On the flesh and blood level it is Rayber, of course, who is the antagonist, and the best indication of O'Connor's intent to lend dramatic balance to her story by rendering this character fully real and plausible is the fact that except for one brief interruption the large middle section of the book, from the evening of Tarwater's arrival through his drowning of Bishop, is developed through the train of thought of Rayber, not Tarwater. Later some of the same incidents of this week are retold, with considerable dramatic effect, from the point of view of Tarwater as we are moved back into his consciousness in Part Three.

In this middle section Rayber is struggling desperately to win the trust of his fiercely ill-tempered and eccentric nephew, whom he earnestly wants to save from being, as he sees it, a freak and a pathetic slave to backwoods ignorance and superstition; he tells the boy that old Tarwater warped everything he touched, that he led a long and useless life and did Tarwater a great injustice. "It's not too late for me to make a man of you!" he says. As Rayber tries to find a way to cope with Tarwater, we see him thinking back over the crises of his own life: his own brief sojourn with old Tarwater as a small boy, when he himself had become a loving devotee of Powderhead; his later growth into mature independence—marked by an irrational lapse, from time to time, into renewed desire for the old man, a yearning to have his fish-colored eyes turned on him again; and his short and bitter marriage to the welfare worker. For this woman and all such secular priests of the modern paternalistic state—Rayber himself is a "testing expert" for the public schools— O'Conner reserves, of course, her deepest scorn. Rayber recalls, in a passage that places considerable strain on the imagination, that his wife had been terrified by a glimpse of the face of the baby Tarwater on the old man's front porch when they had paid their famous call to rescue him; the baby seemed to her to have the face of an adult and one with "immoveable, insane convictions," and when her own child, the defective Bishop, was born, she was dismayed to find that *his* face resembled the old man's. The narrator proves her right about all this, of course, but the point is that she cannot face any of the real truth about life that her involvement with this queer family—and her giving birth to a defective baby—has forced her to confront; she can only flee.

There are passages here where the writer permits the reader to draw close to Rayber and to sympathize with him to a certain extent in his desire to help the boy; the first night Tarwater spends in the house, for instance, we are shown Rayber sitting up all night simply looking at him and dreaming about their future life together.

> The first night he had sat until daylight by the side of the bed where, still dressed, the boy had fallen. He had sat there, his eyes shining, like a man who sits before a treasure he is not yet convinced is real. His eyes had moved over and over the sprawled thin figure which had appeared lost in an exhaustion so profound that it seemed doubtful it would ever move again. As he followed the outline of the face, he had realized with an intense stab of joy that his nephew looked enough like him to be his son. The heavy work shoes, the worn overalls, the atrocious stained hat filled him with pain and pity.

There is also a scene in which Rayber remembers finding out that his own son was a hopeless idiot. His rage that such a thing could be, O'Connor does not mock; the doctor says Rayber should be grateful that the child's health, at least, is good, saying that he had seen them born without arms and legs—and one with a heart outside. Rayber "had lurched up, almost ready to strike the man. 'How can I be grateful,' he had hissed, 'when one—just one?—is born with a heart outside?' " Such scenes—and even these are not, tonally, exactly right—are O'Connor's attempt, of course, to be fair to Rayber; there is a good deal of this, and yet one feels considerable uneasiness about this characterization. It is possible to accept Rayber—given his childhood ordeals and his generally unhappy life—as a weak, damaged, really not very clever individual; but the problem is that the novel needs to have us accept him as something much more important than that. It needs to have us accept his way of life and thought as the major alternative to the religious life, as the representative of the kind of life Tarwater will have to lead if he turns away from Christ for good. O'Connor's own blunt statement of the boy's options was made in an interview a couple of years after the book came out; she said that what she wanted to "get across" in *The Violent Bear It Away* was

"the fact that the great uncle (Old Tarwater) is the
Christian—a sort of crypto-Catholic—and that the schoolteacher (Rayber) is the typical modern man. The boy
(young Tarwater) has to choose which one, which way,
he wants to follow. It's a matter of vocation." [18] As for the
notion of Rayber as "typical modern man"—one has
plenty of one's own scorn to heap on such an idea, and
the casual arrogance of the phrase itself tells its own tale.
The truth is that O'Connor could not begin to do justice
to the humanistic view of life. An interesting exchange
with O'Connor on this same subject was reported in the
*New York Review* by the writer Richard Gilman, who
visited her at the Milledgeville farm in the fall of 1960:

> She suspected that she didn't know the intellectual world,
> and was aware that it had its suspicions of her. She wasn't,
> of course, wholly the product of small-time and rural edu-
> cation and experience: she had attended the University of
> Iowa Writer's Workshop, had spent some time in the East
> with her friends, the Fitzgeralds, and was in touch with
> other writer-friends through correspondence and occasional
> visits. Until the last stages of her illness she made one or
> two trips a year to talk at colleges or conferences. Yet I
> wasn't surprised when she asked me if I thought she had
> "gotten right" the intellectual (Rayber, the teacher) in *The
> Violent Bear It Away*. "I don't reckon he'd be very con-
> vincing to you folks in New York," she said. I said, after
> wondering for a moment where I stood, no, he wasn't a
> very convincing intellectual and, growing bolder, that in fact
> I thought he was one of the few occasions when her art
> failed because she hadn't sacrificed what she thought she
> knew. She was silent and then said she thought I was prob-
> ably right.[19]

The child Bishop is the focus of an aspect of Rayber's
supposedly typical atheistical thought that strikes one as
particularly farfetched—I am referring to Rayber's feel-

18. Joel Wells, "Off the Cuff," *Critic*, XXI (August-September,
1962), 4–5, 71–72.
19. Richard Gilman, in a review of *Mystery and Manners* in *New
York Review of Books*, VIII (August 21, 1969).

ing that he cannot give in to his love for the child without
falling prey to an irrational and abnormal love for all
created things which is the beginning of a mad return to
faith. "For the most part Rayber lived with him [Bishop]
without being painfully aware of his presence but the moments would still come when, rushing from some inex-
plicable part of himself, he would experience a love for
the child so outrageous that he would be left shocked and
depressed for days, and trembling for his sanity." He
hardly dares even to take the child on his lap, and he is
led at one point, in a poorly imagined scene on the beach,
to try to drown him. Loss of faith leads, we are being told,
to a paralysis of the emotions; the atheist opts for the
dignity of emotional death as against what he sees as the
insanity of belief. O'Connor endows Rayber with a certain
amount of ability to understand the deep dilemma of his
nephew—Rayber comes to realize that what Tarwater
himself fears is his mounting urge to baptize Bishop; but
her mockery of Rayber's attempts to seduce Tarwater
with new clothes, toys, and adventures is broadly done,
and another offense is her constant harping on Rayber's
trust in psychological testing. For Rayber an untested
boy is, one might say, a lost boy; he has devised some
special tests of his own that he would like to give to Tarwater—Tarwater violently refuses to take them, of course
—"to ferret to the center of the emotional infection." This
would drive anyone back to Jesus, to be sure.

And as one might expect, on this slippery ground O'Connor loses for long stretches the comic angle so warmly
sustained in Part One. What comic pleasure there is here
derives from the impossibility of Tarwater's and Rayber's
relationship. Tarwater cares nothing for Rayber's pity
and concern and constantly insults and humiliates him.
When he first notices Rayber's hearing aid (one of the
many signs of Rayber's dehumanization—one of Old Tarwater's shotgun blasts had nipped his ear), he says, "What
are you wired for? . . . Does your head light up?" When

Rayber is suddenly struck with the idea of giving Tarwater a thrill by taking an airplane ride, Tarwater says, "I wouldn't give you nothing for no airplane. A buzzard can fly"—and besides, he had been up with the old man. Rayber hopes to overwhelm Tarwater with the wonders of city life, but this is a vain hope if there ever was one:

> They had simply covered . . . the entire city, walking, and all night Rayber rewalked the same territory backwards in his sleep. . . . Tarwater was always slightly in advance of them, pushing forward on the scent of something. In four days they had been to the art gallery and the movies, they had toured department stores, ridden escalators, visited the supermarkets, inspected the water works, the post office, the railroad yards and the city hall. Rayber had explained how the city was run and detailed the duties of a good citizen. He had talked as much as he had walked, and the boy for all the interest he showed might have been the one who was deaf. Silent, he viewed everything with the same noncommittal eye as if he found nothing here worth holding his attention but must keep moving, must keep searching for whatever it was that appeared just beyond his vision.

And here we have, in Tarwater's contemptuous indifference to everything he sees, the whole awesome O'Connor view of human life. This is the tour of our world her writings give us again and again—no matter where one looks, no matter how deep into ordinary human activity, there is nothing worth holding one's attention, nothing of value or interest. Nothing, that is, except pure religious passion. And this passage also brings home to us once again the enormity of what O'Connor is attempting to do with such characters as Tarwater—the enormity of her attempt to render somehow plausible the total asceticism of these country boys.

But in this section of the novel, in any case, the trouble is that the O'Connor doctrine is taking over control of the story in too transparent a way. The rich invention and spontaneity of the Powderhead section are giving way to a too-mechanical working out of the O'Connor formula.

The tendency of the story is to move, without the zest and marvelous conviction of Part One, from symbolic incident to symbolic incident—the sun's sudden illumination, for instance, of the head of the dim-witted child as Tarwater watches him in the pool of a fountain in the park; Rayber's perplexed discovery of Tarwater standing transfixed before an undressed bakery window where lies one forgotten loaf of bread. An almost unbroken succession of such scenes finally overwhelms the reader with a sense that the characters are being more and more fatally trapped in the author's narrow purpose for them—that O'Connor's artistry, however brilliant it could sometimes be, is knuckling under to the evangelist, intent on clearing out all possible ambiguities. Of course there are compelling passages even here; the passage, for instance, which describes Rayber's strangely concentrated secret pursuit of Tarwater through the night-time streets of the town captures Rayber's deep fascination with the mysterious behavior of Tarwater in an eerie way. There is this sharp commentary, for instance, on Rayber's constantly harried self-defeat: half-dressed and barefooted, he crashes into a garbage can in a dark alley—"He scrambled up and limped on, hearing his own curses like the voice of a stranger broadcast through his hearing aid."

The dramatic peak of the Rayber section of the book (Part Two) comes at the end of the section, where our last view of the unhappy man comes as he hears, trying to scan the moonlit lake from the window of his lodge, the death cries of his son as Tarwater drowns him. Rayber has been waiting in his room for the two boys to return from a late afternoon boat ride; he dozes in his chair, exhausted from his failures with Tarwater and dreaming of a means of escape from him. When he wakes, the room is growing dim, and this is what he sees from the window: "The boat with the two of them in it was near the middle of the lake, almost still. They were sitting there facing each other in the isolation of the water, Bishop small and squat, and

Tarwater gaunt, lean, bent slightly forward, his whole attention concentrated on the opposite figure. They seemed to be held still in some magnetic field of attraction. The sky was an intense purple as if it were about to explode into darkness."

Rayber dozes again, thinking of a last ultimatum that he will deliver to Tarwater when he returns; he will say, "Bishop and I are returning tonight. You may go with us under these conditions: not that you begin to cooperate, but that you cooperate, fully and completely, that you change your attitude, that you allow yourself to be tested, that you prepare yourself to enter school in the fall, and that you take that hat [these ubiquitous O'Connor hats!] off your head right now and throw it out the window into the lake." When Rayber wakes again, he sees that the moon, "travelling toward the middle of the window," has lost its color. "The sky," O'Connor writes, "was a hollow black, and an empty road of moonlight crossed the lake." Rayber searches the darkness in vain, but when he turns on his hearing aid, "the machine picked up the sounds of some fierce sustained struggle in the distance." Bishop's screams now reach his ears: "The [last] bellow rose and fell, then it blared out one last time, rising out of its own momentum, as if it were escaping finally, after centuries of waiting, into silence." To have the drowning strained distantly through the darkness and through Rayber's hearing aid artfully muffles in ghostly mystery this crucial event of the story. Rayber intuits, just before he collapses, that Tarwater, drawing the knot of his bitter schizophrenic torment even more tightly about him, has spoken the words of baptism over Bishop even as he drowned him and is now moving off through the dark woods—Powderhead lies nearby—"to meet his appalling destiny."

But this phrase, Tarwater's "appalling destiny," is a reminder that in the Rayber section of the book, in which we see the boy's queer behavior only from a distance, O'Connor is using to the full a favorite narrative strategy

—that of boldly facing and exploiting the "normal" person's view of her religious heroes as freaks and madmen. This was, as we saw, a major device throughout *Wise Blood* and was eminently effective in the opening and closing scenes of the book, where we get the astonished views of Hazel of the two middle-aged women. O'Connor often obtained these contrasts by use of the chance encounter. Indeed the chance encounter is a much used device in both the novels and the short stories as a means of suddenly casting a character into fresh perspective. In some stories, in fact, these chance encounters between oddly matched strangers, meetings that usually turn out to be intensely traumatic for the major character, form the central situation of the piece; there is the meeting, for instance, of the grandmother and the Misfit in "A Good Man Is Hard to Find," of Hulga and the Bible salesman in "Good Country People," and of good-natured Mrs. Turpin and the fierce Wellesleyite of "Revelation."

There are at least three such encounters in *The Violent Bear It Away*: three times Tarwater, going to and from Powderhead, hitches a ride with a stranger. The first two men he meets this way are notable for their ordinariness —it is as if these scenes are in part O'Connor's way of saying, "You see this *is* the real world I'm writing about." Meeks gives Tarwater a banal lesson on the saving value of work and success, but when he says, "What line was your great-uncle in?" the enormous split between the two worlds opens up as Tarwater replies, "He was a prophet," and Meeks's shoulders are said to jump "several times as if they were going to leap over his head." Moving through the night back to Powderhead after drowning Bishop, Tarwater catches his second ride—this time with a tough truckdriver. "You got to keep me awake or you don't ride, buddy," he says. "I ain't picking you up to do you no favor." So Tarwater is forced to speak, and at last the reader hears where the boy thinks he stands after his agonizing week in the city and his terrible deed at the lake:

"How come your pantslegs are wet?" the driver persisted.
"I drowned a boy," Tarwater said.
"Just one?" the driver asked.
"Yes." He reached over and caught hold of the sleeve of the man's shirt. His lips worked a few seconds. They stopped and then started again as if the force of a thought were behind them but no words. He shut his mouth, then tried again but no sound came. Then all at once the sentence rushed out and was gone. "I baptized him."
"Huh?" the man said.
"It was an accident. I didn't mean to," he said breathlessly. Then in a calmer voice he said, "The words just come out of themselves but it don't mean nothing. You can't be born again."
"I only meant to drown him," the boy said. "You're only born once. They were just some words that run out of my mouth and spilled in the water." He shook his head violently as if to scatter his thoughts. "There's nothing where I'm going but the stall," he began again, "because the house is burnt up but that's the way I want it. I don't want nothing of his. Now it's all mine."
"Of his whose?" the man muttered.
"Of my great-uncle's," the boy said. "I'm going back there. I ain't going to leave it again. I'm in full charge there. No voice will be uplifted. I shouldn't never have left it except I had to prove I wasn't no prophet and I've proved it." He paused and jerked the man's sleeve. "I proved it by drowning him. Even if I did baptize him that was only an accident. Now all I have to do is mind my own bidnis until I die. I don't have to baptize or prophesy."

Thus Tarwater unburdens himself of his bizarre history; and this is all the response he gets or—symbolically speaking—may ever get: "That don't make sense but make up some more of it. I gotta stay awake." When Tarwater says he is hungry but then is unable to eat the sandwich the man gives him, the man says, "I don't want you puking in here and if you got something catching, you get out right now." The driver later sums up, in effect, the reactions of a number of readers to O'Connor's fanatical heroes: "You belong in the booby hatch," he tells Tarwater. "You ride through these states and you see they all belong in it. I won't see nobody sane again until I get back to Detroit."

But Tarwater does not stand, even now, where he says —and tries to believe—he stands, and his third encounter, a very different one, supplies the final shock that begins to bring him to his senses (or takes him completely out of them, according to one's point of view). The next morning Tarwater is picked up by a stranger in a lavender and cream-colored car, and suddenly the novel leads us into a very strange world indeed, where every nightmarish detail is fraught with symbolic meaning. When Tarwater turns to look at the man who has picked him up, "an unpleasant sensation that he could not place came over him." But the reader knows why Tarwater reacts as he does— this diabolic character is the very image of the sweet-voiced "stranger" who has been luring the boy away from his Christian mission all through the novel: "The person who had picked him up was a pale, lean, old-looking young man with deep hollows under his cheekbones. He had on a lavender shirt and a thin black suit and a panama hat. His lips were as white as the cigaret that hung limply from one side of his mouth. His eyes were the same color as his shirt and were ringed with heavy black lashes. A lock of yellow hair fell across his forehead from under his pushed-back hat."

The man drugs the boy with tobacco and liquor (of the liquor Tarwater says, "It's better than the Bread of Life"), and when he passes out, completes the corruption of the flesh by assaulting him in the woods. As souvenirs he takes Tarwater's hat (the remnant of his life at Powderhead) and his corkscrew-bottleopener (Rayber's gift and the sign of Tarwater's attempted rebellion: "This here thing will open anything," he had told the driver). When Tarwater comes to, he is lying propped against a log, naked except for his shoes, his hands tied behind him with the lavender handkerchief. This is O'Connor's description of his face as he first realizes what has happened to him:

> The boy's mouth twisted open and to the side as if it were going to displace itself permanently. In a second it appeared to be only a gap that would never be a mouth again. His eyes looked small and seedlike as if while he was asleep, they had been lifted out, scorched, and dropped back into his head. His expression seemed to contract until it reached some point beyond rage or pain. Then a loud cry tore out of him and his mouth fell back into place.
>
> He began to tear savagely at the lavender handkerchief until he had shredded it off. Then he got into his clothes so quickly that when he finished he had half of them on backwards and did not notice.

Tarwater then sets fire to the place where the foul act had been done and sets off again for Powderhead, knowing that now "he could not turn back," that "his destiny forced him on to a final revelation."

But I am afraid the reader is bound to watch all this from rather a cool distance, less dismayed by the fate of the boy than by the lapse of authorial discretion. The rape episode is one of the most problematic in O'Connor's work. This is not to say that it is problematic in terms of what the action signifies, of its technical function in the novel; that is clear enough: its purpose is to show that Tarwater has felt the full horror of the embrace of evil and has instinctively recoiled in bitter anger and disgust. But on the affective level, the power of this scene is dim indeed. In the first place, the author takes little trouble to try to put her macabre rapist across as a literal possibility. The reader has little choice but to regard him, not as simply a diabolic figure, but as the devil himself come down to complete the job of Tarwater's subjugation. His resemblance to the original "stranger" who had begun the seduction of the boy at old Tarwater's death goes far beyond mere coincidence and is clearly not presented as a trick of Tarwater's imagination. After the rape, for instance, the author herself steps forward to describe the rapist as he leaves the scene: "In about an hour the stranger emerged alone and looked furtively about him. He was carrying the boy's hat for a souvenir and also the corkscrew-bottle-opener. His delicate skin had acquired a faint pink tint as if he had refreshed himself on blood. He got quickly into his car and sped away." One may make much of O'Connor's *as if* in this passage, but this is a very meager subjunctive indeed. The fact is that the scene is artificial and melodramatic and choked with the overwrought symbolism which is more or less a problem all through Parts Two and Three of the book and which comes close here to turning the whole action into wooden puppetry.

Thus the mounting aggravations of the latter half of *The Violent Bear It Away* expand here to crisis proportions; this is the point at which the novel seems to come unmoored from its vibrantly lifelike beginnings at Powderhead in Part One. Certainly part of the problem is that O'Connor could not continue to keep her hero plausibly suspended on the teetering pole of his torturous indecision, that she was beginning to exhaust the resources of her situation for showing this struggle in recognizable human terms.

In fact the nervous ambivalence that one is prone to feel about the value of O'Connor's work is perhaps more acutely felt in this section of her second novel than anywhere else in her work—the admixture, that is, of good and bad elements is particularly frustrating. But I will give one further example of what I mean. Like Lawrence, O'Connor had an unusual gift for using the natural world as a means of reflecting and epitomizing a character's inner struggle; the use of nature in this way is not so much a technique as it is an ability to capitalize on a habit of the mind or imagination that we are all to some extent familiar with. We all know how, in times of fear and distress, the mind plays tricks and things outside seem, not only to be full of signs and portents, but to be active agents in the battles we fight within. And while it was O'Connor's excessive concentration on this habit of mind that accounts for much of the overly systematized allegory of Tarwater's battle of conscience, she could also use this tendency of the boy's imagination in a quite natural, restrained, and psychologically plausible way. In Part One, for instance, she is describing Tarwater's terrified awakening from his drunken sleep in the cove the night of the old man's death:

> Some night bird complaining close by woke him up. It was not a screeching noise, only an intermittent hump-hump as if the bird had to recall his grievance each time before he repeated it. Clouds were moving convulsively across a black sky and there was a pink unsteady moon that appeared to be jerked up a foot or so and then dropped and jerked up again. This was because, as he observed in an instant, the sky was lowering, coming down fast to smother him. The bird screeched and flew off in time and Tarwater lurched into the middle of the stream bed and crouched on his hands and knees. The moon was reflected like pale fire in the few spots of water in the sand. He sprang at the wall of honeysuckle and began to tear through it, confusing the sweet familiar odor with the weight coming down on him. When he stood up on the other side, the black ground swung slowly and threw him down again. A flare of pink lightning lit the woods and he saw the black shapes of trees pierce out of the ground all around him. The night bird began to hump again from a thicket where he had settled.

As Tarwater moves back to Powderhead at the end of the book, his sense of the expressiveness of the natural world reaches a new height. Everything around him seems to take on some awesome significance—it is as if he moves in a world of ghosts. The ground he walks on seems to him like "a giant beast which might at any moment stretch a muscle and send him rolling into the ditch below." Well water in which he bathes his face seems to be bewitched, and he thinks he sees in it two silent eyes gazing at him. A woman storekeeper looks to him like an avenging angel:

"There was all knowledge in her stony face and the fold of her arms indicated a judgment fixed from the foundations of time. Huge wings might have been folded behind her without seeming strange." As he looks down on the clearing—on the burnt ruins of the house framed by the old man's beloved fields—the sound of a wood thrush affects him like a key being turned in his heart. The "encroaching dusk" seems to "come softly in deference to some mystery" residing in the clearing. And as he approaches, the field beyond looks to him like the field where Jesus fed the multitude from the basket of loaves and fishes. One can certainly go too far in endowing characters with such sensations as these—Lawrence clearly went too far in this direction at times—but some of the most expressive writing in both of these writers is also attained in just this way.

But as we try to reckon the successes and failures of the book, where do we place the final scene, the most soaringly lyrical passage in O'Connor's work, in which Tarwater, on the sacred ground of Powderhead, at last surrenders himself to the religious vision of his old uncle? One can sympathize, to some extent, with readers who have felt that the scene is evasive. What exactly, one may ask, is Tarwater doing as he sets yet another fire? Is he burning up the whole woods? And are we to assume that he will now live forever in an ecstasy of religious passion and self-debasement? And what about Tarwater's crimes? One reader has even put the question—Where are the police around here anyway? "Doubtless there are asylums for the criminally insane even in Georgia," wrote a reviewer of this novel in the *Hudson Review*, "though murder, mayhem, kidnapping and arson have not aroused the curiosity of a single policeman throughout the book." [20] But it seems to me that O'Connor's rhetoric here does

20. Vivian Mercier, "Sex, Success, and Salvation," *Hudson Review*, XIII (Autumn, 1960), 454–55.

work its spell and that such questions do not really intrude
as one reads.

Tarwater's increasing awareness of the mysterious silence, the mounting pain of his hunger, his growing faith
in the purifying power of fire, and the shock of discovery
when he wakes after the ordeal of the traveler, whom he
himself comes to identify with the voice of the pursuing
"stranger"—all of these things now work powerfully in
him to effect the end of his rebellion. When his vision
sweeps across the scene of his life with the old man once
more, he hears the whisper of the stranger again, a
"sibilant shifting of the air" dropping "like a sigh into
his ear," telling him to go down and claim his property.
"It's ours," the stranger says; "we've won it." But now
the voice only sickens Tarwater, he is enraged by this
"grinning presence" and plunges a burning pine bough
into the forked tree from which the voice seems to ema-
nate. As the flames rise up, the fire seems to form a wall
between him and the grinning presence. And Tarwater's
spirits rise as he sees that his foe will soon be consumed
by the roaring fire.

The final intuition of his divine role comes to the boy
as he moves into the clearing and sees that old Tarwater's
grave has been prepared by the Negro Buford, who appears at the graveside as the boy approaches. "The grave,
freshly mounded, lay between them. Tarwater lowered
his eyes to it. At its head, a dark rough cross was set
starkly in the bare ground. The boy's hands opened stiffly
as if he were dropping something he had been clutching
all his life." So the war of Tarwater's contending angels
is over, and he is overwhelmed by the full wonderful significance of his hunger and all the succession of strange
sensations of the divine presence.

Seen in the context of modern experience and belief, one
thing is clear: that this audacious book gives us, at its
best, something that is all the more valuable because
in modern writing it is so rare—a sense of what it is like,

what it feels like, to believe that Christian belief means everything and is a matter of life and death, even of eternal life and eternal death. And going back to the unquestionably fine writing in the opening part of this queer tale, one must also remember to credit the writer with the creation of one deeply engaging and vivid character. And it is fitting that near the end of the book it is an image of the old man—as seen now by what, in the authorial view at least, are the truth-blistered eyes of the boy—that stirs the reader into at least momentary fusion with the fundamental aim of the novel and with O'Connor's religious vision: the boy's illusion of seeing the old man being lowered to the basket of loaves and fishes, leaning impatiently forward to partake of the blessed food. "The boy too leaned forward, aware at last of the object of his hunger, aware that it was the same as the old man's and that nothing on earth would fill him." But let the final words of the novel speak for themselves:

> He stood there, straining forward, but the scene faded in the gathering darkness. Night descended until there was nothing but a thin streak of red between it and the black line of earth but still he stood there. He felt his hunger no longer as a pain but as a tide. He felt it rising in himself through time and darkness, rising through the centuries, and he knew that it rose in a line of men whose lives were chosen to sustain it, who would wander in the world, strangers from that violent country where the silence is never broken except to shout the truth. He felt it building from the blood of Abel to his own, rising and engulfing him. It seemed in one instant to lift and turn him. He whirled toward the treeline. There, rising and spreading in the night, a red-gold tree of fire ascended as if it would consume the darkness in one tremendous burst of flame. The boy's breath went out to meet it. He knew that this was the fire that had encircled Daniel, that had raised Elijah from the earth, that had spoken to Moses and would in the instant speak to him. He threw himself to the ground and with his face against the dirt of the grave, he heard the command. GO WARN THE CHILDREN OF GOD OF THE TERRIBLE SPEED OF MERCY. The

words were as silent as seeds opening one at a time in his blood.

When finally he raised himself, the burning bush had disappeared. A line of fire ate languidly at the treeline and here and there a thin crest of flame rose farther back in the woods where a dull red cloud of smoke had gathered. The boy stooped and picked up a handful of dirt off his great-uncle's grave and smeared it on his forehead. Then after a moment, without looking back he moved across the far field and off the way Buford had gone.

By midnight he had left the road and the burning woods behind him and had come out on the highway once more. The moon, riding low above the field beside him, appeared and disappeared, diamond-bright, between patches of darkness. Intermittently the boy's jagged shadow slanted across the road ahead of him as if it cleared a rough path toward his goal. His singed eyes, black in their clear sockets, seemed already to envision the fate that awaited him but he moved steadily on, his face set toward the dark city, where the children of God lay sleeping.

Chapter IV

# The Short Stories

It is a pleasure to turn finally to a part of O'Connor's work
about which one need express few serious reservations:
that is, to some nine or ten nearly perfect short stories. To
admire these stories is, of course, easy enough; to plumb
the secrets of their art difficult indeed. This final chapter
will attempt critiques of three of this remarkable set.
From the first volume we will examine O'Connor's two
earliest attempts to turn to artistic use, after her return
to Milledgeville, the life that she and her mother began
to live on Andalusia Farm—"A Temple of the Holy
Ghost" and "A Circle in the Fire." The first of these,
which is about a strangely evoked crisis in a young girl's
secret religious life, is not only a fine story in its own right
but one with this special interest: it seems to tell us something about O'Connor's own childhood, about how the
mind of the formidable narrator of all these bizarre tales
was formed. "A Circle in the Fire," a vibrant story perfectly rounded in a traditional but deeply satisfying way,
tells of the invasion of a widow's farm by three mischievous—but in some awesome way more than mischievous—
urchins from the city. The third story, "Parker's Back,"
comes from the second collection, *Everything That Rises
Must Converge,* and from the group of tales in which
O'Connor deals, as in her novels, with southern poor
whites; this is the tale about the tattooed Christ on O. E.
Parker's back.

When we put all the O'Connor short stories together

144

(and counting the early Iowa stories included in *The Complete Stories* there are twenty-six of them), we find that we can sort them out, arrange and categorize them in an almost endless number of ways, all of these ways more or less interesting, perhaps, but most of them hardly more than incidental to the crucial critical questions which must be raised about their art. The O'Connor stories are a closely knit body of stories in the sense that they overlap each other in a thick network of repeated themes, situations, narrative strategies and patterns, and of Dickens-like detail as to southern speech and manners. And if, in fact, we cannot quite consider these stories, taken altogether, to constitute a truly first-rate body of short fiction, it is partly because they are too closely knit and overlapping, in both large and minor ways. They tend, in other words, to blend into each other rather too well, to become rather too predictable—charming surprises in the early stories one reads come to seem finally almost like O'Connor clichés. And what is probably even more important is that, as I suggested in the first chapter of this study, when one takes the stories altogether, the relentlessly narrow O'Connor view of human affairs tends to weigh on the reader much more heavily, to come much closer—than any one story taken separately—to a falsification of human experience as most of us know it.

And similarly, when one compares the stories to the novels, one realizes that one reason why many of the individual stories are more successful than the novels is that O'Connor's formidable, often unreasonable doctrine about human life is generally not pushed in any one story beyond the bounds of common sense—one knows how O'Connor herself would have despised such a term— the way it is pushed in the novels. In this respect O'Connor is much like D. H. Lawrence: the closer Lawrence came to full development of his ideas and theories on life —centering, generally, in his case, on ideal relations between men and women—the more unreasonable he could seem, the more exasperatingly domineering. A short story, of course, does not permit of this full development, can do no more than sound a suggestive bar of it; the feeling for life that lies behind the doctrine and the theories has to serve, and in both these writers often did serve wonderfully well.

One might say, also, about the sameness and repetitiveness of O'Connor's fiction that her forced exile on the Milledgeville farm worked against her (it doubtless had certain advantages as well) in one important way: it constricted her range of subjects rather too much; her imagination fed greedily on everything that fell within her immediate purview but was hard put to leap much beyond. Is there any O'Connor reader who was not disappointed with the excerpt from what would have been her third novel?[1] This passage is thoroughly, consistently repetitive of material she had already worked and reworked and worked again. The narrowness of her doctrine seems to have combined with the narrowness of her physical life to produce an art that was highly static, if often enormously skillful.

About O'Connor's private life there is still much to be puzzled over. Judging by the many conflicting attempts to evoke the true Flannery O'Connor, it seems that O'Connor biography will be a difficult chore, partly because of the style of southern life—where things are never what they seem to be—in the class in which she and her mother lived. One reads, on the one hand, that Miss O'Connor was a loving daughter, known for her warmth and friendliness —on the other, that she was strange and aloof, a trial to her family and friends. About her inner life and the way

1. This brief excerpt, titled "Why Do the Heathens Rage?" first appeared in *Esquire* in July, 1963. It is reprinted in *The Complete Stories*. The plan for this novel and several hundred pages of rough, fragmentary material are on file at the Georgia College Library. For a description of the papers in Milledgeville, see an article by Gerald Becham in a new journal, *The Flannery O'Connor Bulletin*, published annually in Milledgeville.

she really felt about things around her her fiction itself
will probably continue to tell us more than what we will
learn about her daily affairs and relationships in such
places as Savannah, Milledgeville, Iowa, and Connecticut.
As a very young writer, we do know that O'Connor
wasted no time settling down to what would be her lifelong fictional subject: life amongst the various classes of
people in or around Milledgeville, verging at times, as in
*The Violent Bear It Away,* into the North Georgia and
Tennessee hills and always with not only "the town" and
the countryside, but also "the city"—often named or
identifiable as Atlanta—as a fixed referent in her geogra-
phy and at times the main scene of the action.

Her fascination with backwoods country people is already apparent in three of the six stories submitted at
Iowa for her master's thesis. She wrote, as we have seen,
about the painful trip of the country youth Hazel Wickers
from his native village to the alien city, and in "The
Geranium" about the old redneck Dudley miserably
stranded in an apartment in New York; in a story called
"Wildcat" she wrote about an old Negro (the only O'Connor tale with a Negro protagonist) who believes, as indeed
the reader comes to believe—the story owes perhaps too
much to Faulkner's "That Evening Sun Go Down"—that
he can smell a wildcat lying in the woods near his shack
waiting to attack him. The boy Ruller in "The Capture" is
a town boy, but his turkey is stolen by some country youths
who accost him on his way home from the outlying woods.
O'Connor put the Milledgeville teachers' college in one
story—in a rather poorly focused tale ("The Barber")
about a young professor who ineptly argues Georgia poli-
tics with the locals in the town barbershop. And in the
sixth of these stories she tells a somewhat livelier tale
about a spinster writer, or would-be writer, whose impossible story about a young dirt farmer comes suddenly to
life in her fantasies as she herself enters the story as the
farmer's devoted wife. The towns which these stories are

laid in or near are given names which, almost without exception, are modulations on the name Milledgeville: Mayville, Melton, Melsy, Dilton, Tilford, Willahobie.

In the early chapters of *Wise Blood* which followed the Iowa stories O'Connor's southern rural milieu—in this book country people living in the city—is seen at its most savage. And with the *Wise Blood* pieces comes a story about another exile from "around Melsy," Ruby Hill of "A Woman on the Stair," or as the tale was later retitled, "A Stroke of Good Fortune," the first of O'Connor's stories to be included in *A Good Man Is Hard to Find.* Ruby's native village Pitman has been abandoned, has simply disappeared off the map just like Hazel's, but she has had the relative good fortune to marry Bill B. Hill, a man from Florida who sells Miracle Products, and to move to Atlanta, where we see her at age thirty-five making the terrifying discovery that she is pregnant.

Between this story and the next, four years elapsed, during which O'Connor finished *Wise Blood* in Connecticut (living with the Fitzgeralds), was struck by the lupus, and recuperated back home in Milledgeville. In 1953 the much funnier and fiercer O'Connor stories began with a vengeance—her settings more or less unchanged—with "A Good Man Is Hard to Find"; the amazing essay in tall rural humor, O'Connor's first fully successful story, "The Life You Save May Be Your Own"; the more gently religious story "The River"; and a story which is one of the neglected masterpieces of the first collection, "A Late Encounter with the Enemy." In this story O'Connor used the Milledgeville college—ingloriously, of course, like nearly everything else—for the second and last time; this is a tale about a senile old man who dies, dressed up in his fake confederate general's uniform, in his wheelchair on stage during the college graduation exercises where his sixty-four-year-old daughter is getting her B.S. This story, with an almost breathless succession of fine comic touches, is every bit as funny a story as "A Good Man Is

Hard to Find," but it is also a tale (and one of the very earliest) in which O'Connor succeeds in bringing her radically diverse tonal elements into harmony. We have, in other words, a hilariously comic story of an almost tall tale variety, but one which also slyly and carefully builds to a startlingly eerie climax: as the old man is overtaken by death, his memory flashes to life again and his whole past, asleep so long in his one-hundred-and-four-year-old mind, rushes upon him. The final image of the story is a fine stroke indeed; no one but the reader knows that the old man has died during the ceremonies, and at the end we see the corpse in its wheelchair, wheeled by the Boy Scout John Wesley, waiting in line at the Coca-Cola machine.

Now none of O'Connor's stories up to this point contain much of anything very close to O'Connor's private life, though of course they all use, as we have seen, the town and region she knew best and doubtless certain local incidents and characters. The humbling religious experience of the boy in "The Capture" may, of course, encompass something of O'Connor's religious feeling as a child, and the story about the spinster writer may have been an oblique parodistic projection of what a young woman writer of twenty-one or twenty-two half surmised life had in store for *her*. But these are oblique uses of autobiography indeed, and the situation was to change rather radically when the author took up her writing at the Milledgeville farm in the early fifties.

"A Circle in the Fire" appeared in the *Kenyon Review* in the spring of 1954. It features a widow and her daughter living on just such a farm as the O'Connors': the house is a two-story house with a wide screened front porch, farm buildings in back, a wide lawn in front stretching across to a field and then to the fortress line of trees that appears over and over—as Fitzgerald puts it, "like a signature"—in the stories to follow. Essentially the same farm forms the setting for "The Displaced Person," "Good

Country People," "Greenleaf," "A View of the Woods," and "The Enduring Chill."

Moreover, the child in "A Circle in the Fire" is the precursor of a long line of similar children growing up with just such a mother, though not always on a farm, sometimes in town or city; all these sons and daughters —and generally they are grown up bachelors and spinsters—belong, for all their external differences, to a common type: they are sullen, ill-tempered individuals eaten up with a barely suppressed rage which often explodes against their one parent but really seems to encompass everything. Tough and smart in many ways, these rebellious and aggrieved children are nevertheless childishly dependent on their mothers, and in many respects—as, in some stories, the reader only gradually comes to realize —inferior to them, for all their mothers' banal and hypocritical ways, their cliché-ridden thought and speech, and their own particular penchant for seeing themselves as victims and martyrs. The twelve-year-old daughter of "The Circle in the Fire," for instance, sulking and snarling around the house in grotesque tomboy attire, is a trial to her mother in every way—a deep embarrassment to the bravely coping Mrs. Cope, who, referring to her hired man's wife, makes a truly despairing admission for a southern gentlewoman: "Sometimes you look like you might belong to Mrs. Pritchard." As one studies the grim face Miss O'Connor invariably presented to photographers over the years and her amazingly ugly self-portrait, in which her cruelly penetrating gaze is made to match that of the pea hen drawn alongside her, one may well call to mind the habitual exhortation of another of these O'Connor widows afflicted with an unlovely, sour-faced daughter —Mrs. Hopewell, that is, of "Good Country People," who is always reminding poor Hulga-Joy that "a smile never hurt anyone" and that there is nothing wrong with her face that "a pleasant expression wouldn't help."

In spite of the many attempts of O'Connor friends both

inside and outside Milledgeville to foster an image of the
O'Connor household entirely different from this—an image of a loving and dutiful daughter, a selfless and
understanding mother—it would not take a very shrewd
observer to guess, even without benefit of the harsher
O'Connor anecdotes that slip through the less guarded
reminiscences,[2] that O'Connor's widow stories do indeed
reflect—though it is only fair to say they often burlesque
—her own life at Andalusia.

Like Hulga, who makes it plain to her mother that if it
were not for her weak heart she would be "far from these
red hills and good country people," O'Connor must have
felt herself trapped (for she had not chosen, when she
had the choice to make, to make her life in Georgia) in
her mother's care and in the outrageous surface sweetness
of Milledgeville society; and what was doubtless a more
than ordinary streak of native contrariness seems to have
been brought by her forced exile there to full perfection
—certainly in her art, even if not in her life. O'Connor
had her ways of coping with Milledgeville life, and one
can be sure that one of these ways was simply to shut out
whatever became unbearable. Nothing is more vividly, expertly described in her stories than this ability on the part
of the sons and daughters to retreat glumly into themselves. Here are Hulga and Mrs. Hopewell, for instance,
at the breakfast table:

> Nothing is perfect. This was one of Mrs. Hopewell's
> favorite sayings. Another was: that is life! And still an-
> other, the most important, was: well, other people have
> their opinions too. She would make these statements, usu-
> ally at the table, in a tone of gentle insistence as if no one
> held them but her, and the large hulking Joy, whose con-
> stant outrage had obliterated every expression from her
> face, would stare just a little to the side of her, her eyes icy

2. See, for instance, an account of the autograph tea given for
Miss O'Connor when *Wise Blood* appeared: Margaret Inman
Meaders, "Flannery O'Connor: Literary Witch," *Colorado Quar-
terly*, X (Spring, 1962), 377–86.

blue, with the look of someone who had achieved blindness by an act of will and means to keep it.

In "Everything that Rises Must Converge" Julian and his mother are taking that disastrous bus ride, and the mother's conversation with another woman on the bus has driven Julian to shield himself behind a newspaper. "He wants to write but he's selling typewriters until he gets started," his mother is telling the other woman; and the woman replies, "Well that's nice. Selling typewriters is close to writing. He can go right from one to another."

> Behind the newspaper Julian was withdrawing into the inner compartment of his mind where he spent most of his time. This was a kind of mental bubble in which he established himself when he could not bear to be part of what was going on around him. From it he could see out and judge but in it he was safe from any kind of penetration from without. It was the only place where he felt free of the general idiocy of his fellows. His mother had never entered it but from it he could see her with absolute clarity.

(With how little clarity Julian does see his mother—or himself—it is, of course, part of the purpose of this marvelously constructed story to reveal.) And this is the plight of Thomas in "The Comforts of Home": "His mother's behavior throughout the meal was so idiotic that he could barely stand to look at her and since he could less stand to look at Sarah Ham [the young tramp his mother has befriended], he fixed on the sideboard across the room a continuous gaze of disapproval and disgust."

There is a passage in "A Circle in the Fire" which catches in a particularly clever way the mutual exasperation of these comically contrasted pairs, who live a kind of *huit clos* existence, destined to torment each other until doomsday:

> Mrs. Cope was always worrying about fires in her woods. When the nights were very windy, she would say to the child, "Oh Lord, do pray there won't be any fires, it's so windy," and the child would grunt from behind her book

or not answer at all because she heard it so often. In the evenings in the summer when they sat on the porch, Mrs. Cope would say to the child who was reading fast to catch the last light, "Get up and look at the sunset, it's gorgeous. You ought to get up and look at it," and the child would scowl and not answer or glare up once across the lawn and two front pastures to the gray-blue sentinel line of trees and then begin to read again with no change of expression, sometimes muttering for meanness, "It looks like a fire. You better get up and smell around and see if the woods ain't on fire."

It is on this porch that Mrs. McIntyre tells the priest she has decided to let the displaced person go (and that the priest, looking out onto the lawn where a peacock is spreading his wondrous tail, says, "Christ will come like that!") ; and it is on this porch that in "The Enduring Chill," Mrs. Fox torments Asbury in the evenings by trying to talk about things that interest him : "When you get well, I think it would be nice if you wrote a book about down here. We need another good book like *Gone With the Wind*."

And about that wall of trees that could be seen from the porch across the fields—to what marvelously varied use O'Connor was able to put them in her stories! To Asbury (of the story just mentioned), who is about to experience the shock of purifying terror that will finally mark the beginning for him of a new life, the tree-line looks, from his bedroom window, black against the crimson sky; and it seems to him to form "a brittle wall, standing as if it were the frail defense he had set up in his mind to protect him from what was coming." For Mrs. May in "Greenleaf" the tree-line is also a fortress—she thinks of it as protecting her property from assaults from outside; but she dreams that the sun is trying to burn through the tree-line, and just as she is feeling "safe in the knowledge that it couldn't, that it had to sink the way it always did outside her property," it turns from a swollen red ball to a bullet, narrow and pale, and (foreshadowing Mrs. May's

death on the horns of the bull) it seems in her dream to
"burst through the tree line and race down the hill toward
her." One of the stories in the second collection turns on
an old man's decision to sell the "lawn"—it is as wide as
a field—to a man who wants to put a gas station on it.
The problem is, the rest of the family try to tell him, that
if the station is built they won't be able to see the line of
woods from the house. Lying alone in his room one afternoon, old Mr. Fortune gets up from time to time from
his bed to stare out the window at these woods, trying to
fathom their mysterious attraction for his family, and
this is his peculiar and intriguing vision:

> The third time he got up to look at the woods, it was al-
> most six o'clock and the gaunt trunks appeared to be raised
> in a pool of red light that gushed from the almost hidden
> sun setting behind them. The old man stared for some time,
> as if for a prolonged instant he were caught up out of the
> rattle of everything that led to the future and were held
> there in the midst of an uncomfortable mystery that he had
> not apprehended before. He saw it, in his hallucination, as
> if someone were wounded behind the woods and the trees
> were bathed in blood.

It would be a simple matter to expand this inventory
of the various ways in which O'Connor recreated from
story to story specific features of the physical and moral
landscape of her own life, but that would not be strictly
to our purpose; we can proceed to a discussion of "A Temple of the Holy Ghost," the first of two tales that we will
examine from the widow-child set of stories we have been
discussing. "A Temple of the Holy Ghost" is not only a
fine story in itself and one that, like "A Late Encounter
with the Enemy," has had less attention than it deserves,
but it is also likely to prove a uniquely interesting piece
as students of O'Connor attempt to discover how her fiction arose out of the experience and circumstances of her
life.

## 2

In one respect it is true to say that O'Connor wrote very little that was personal and autobiographical in the deepest sense. Although one can be sure that her writing gave her, among other things, a means of scourging and punishing herself along with everything else—her own mean and prideful ways—it is also true that she spared herself as a subject in several fundamental respects. That is, what she used in her fiction—what in herself, one might say, she made a public study of—were the negative, grotesque, comical features of her character, her domestic situation, and her relationship with her mother. She never wrote, for instance, about a son or daughter who was a real writer, a gifted, successful writer; in several cases her children are trying to be writers, but they are all failures at whatever it is they do. And further, she never endowed any of her grown children with true Christian belief, although, like nearly all her protagonists, they are usually closer to some kind of religious understanding or belief at the ends of their harrowing tales than they are in the beginning. But in other words, though these fatherless sons and daughters have the manners and temperament of Flannery herself, they are also radically un-O'Connor in that they belong to the secular, other world from which she was so bitterly separated.

"A Temple of the Holy Ghost," however, may well be an exception to all of this. The twelve-year-old heroine of this tale is one of the more intriguing figures of the O'Connor fictional drama in that she is a child that one can imagine growing up to be, not merely one of the grown-child protagonists, but the narrator of these bizarre tales herself. It is difficult to imagine any childhood for a person so odd and eccentric as O'Connor, yet here is one that is perfectly plausible. It certainly does not matter whether the central incident related in this story

—the cousins' account of what the hermaphrodite said at
the fair—was something that happened to O'Connor herself, nor whether anything told here can be linked to
events in her own life; for what is of interest is the nature of the extremely private and secretive inner life of
the young heroine.

It is easy to underestimate this story as one reads
through *A Good Man Is Hard to Find*—it is a quite mild
and unaggressive story compared to the calamitous tales
that accompany it, but it is a tale that seems stronger each
time you return to it. It is a funny story in many clever
ways; all the minor characters are rather gently mocked
except for the mother, who is certainly the most genial
and attractive of the O'Connor widows. The story is one
of the most streamlined as to point of view; the point of
view is always unequivocally the child's, so that it is the
child's sense of the comedy of the people around her—a
comic sense that she realizes borders on sheer meanness
and pridefulness—that is one of the prime subjects of the
story. Her sense of the comedy and absurdity of life has
not grown really vicious yet—the narrator is quite in-
dulgent of what the child sees as her faults—but still it
gives promise of considerable future growth. Consider,
for instance, this Dickens-like portrait of Mr. Cheatam;
the child has just suggested Mr. Cheatam as companion
for her teenage girl cousins who are on a weekend visit
from the convent:

[Miss Kirby] was a long-faced blonde schoolteacher who
boarded with them and Mr. Cheatam was her admirer, a
rich old farmer who arrived every Saturday afternoon in
a fifteen-year-old baby-blue Pontiac powdered with red clay
dust and black inside with Negroes that he charged ten
cents apiece to bring into town on Saturday afternoons.
After he dumped them he came to see Miss Kirby, always
bringing a little gift—a bag of boiled peanuts or a water-
melon or a stalk of sugar cane and once a wholesale box of
Baby Ruth candy bars. He was bald-headed except for a
little fringe of rust-colored hair and his face was nearly the

same color as the unpaved roads and washed like them with ruts and gulleys. He wore a pale green shirt with a thin black stripe in it and blue galluses and his trousers cut across a protruding stomach that he pressed tenderly from time to time with his big flat thumb. All his teeth were backed with gold and he would roll his eyes at Miss Kirby in an impish way and say, "Haw haw," sitting in their porch swing with his legs spread apart and his high-topped shoes pointing in opposite directions on the floor.

The humorless Miss Kirby says, "I don't think Cheat is going to be in town this weekend"; and at this "the child was convulsed afresh, threw herself backward in her chair, fell out of it, rolled on the floor and lay there heaving." Her mother tells her to stop this foolishness or leave the table.

And this is the way the child is about everything around her—people strike her as so ridiculous that she either convulses in laughter or blows up in rage. Her fourteen-year-old cousins, walking around the house in their high heels, "always passing the long mirror in the hall slowly to get a look at their legs," she watches "suspiciously from a distance": "None of their ways were lost on the child." For her they are "practically morons," and she observes that all their sentences begin, "You know this boy I know well one time he. . . ."

These cousins are indeed deftly done—they are just normal, rather empty-headed girls—and the opening sentence of the story first gives us the link that is to pull the whole story together. It is a link between, on the one hand, the girls and their rather ordinary thoughtlessness about serious things, which is needed to set in relief the dire inner seriousness of the child, and on the other the crucial, vibrant words of the hermaphrodite which they will hear at the fair: "All week end the two girls were calling each other Temple One and Temple Two, shaking with laughter and getting so red and hot that they were positively ugly." Later, at table, the mother asks the girls why they call each other Temple One and Temple Two, and O'Connor, expertly catching the pattern of adolescent speech, deepens the contrast between the child and her cousins and gives further development to the central motif of the story:

> Finally they managed to explain. Sister Perpetua, the oldest nun at the Sisters of Mercy in Mayville, had given them a lecture on what to do if a young man should—here they laughed so hard they were not able to go on without going back to the beginning—on what to do if a young man should —they put their heads in their laps—on what to do if— they finally managed to shout it out—if he should "behave in an ungentlemanly manner with them in the back of an automobile." Sister Perpetua said they were to say, "Stop sir! I am a Temple of the Holy Ghost!" and that would put an end to it. The child sat up off the floor with a blank face. She didn't see anything so funny in this. What was really funny was the idea of Mr. Cheatam or Alonzo Myers beau- ing them around. That killed her.
>
> Her mother didn't laugh at what they had said. "I think you girls are pretty silly," she said. "After all, that's what you are—Temples of the Holy Ghost."
>
> The two of them looked up at her, politely concealing their giggles, but with astonished faces as if they were beginning to realize that she was made of the same stuff as Sister Perpetua.

Perhaps the child is hearing this Christian image for the first time; she repeats the sentence to herself—"I am a Temple of the Holy Ghost"—and is pleased with the phrase. "It made her feel as if somebody had given her a present." And later she reflects about the poor spinster Miss Kirby: "And she's a Temple of the Holy Ghost, too."

The child finally makes to her mother a serious proposal for entertaining her cousins—to enlist the farm youths Wendell and Cory; she has heard that they are both going to be "Church of God preachers because you don't have to know nothing to be one." But she tells her cousins that the boys are real dreamboats, and when they appear that night, she hides in the bushes by the porch to see what happens. The boys play and sing country religious music, the girls trying not to laugh, and then the girls sing "with their convent-trained voices" *Tantum ergo Sacramentum.* When they finish, one of the boys says, "That must be Jew singing," and the child can contain her massive contempt no longer: " 'You big dumb ox!' she shouted. 'You big dumb Church of God ox!' she roared and fell off the barrel and scrambled up and shot around the corner of the house as they jumped from the banister to see who was shouting."

The two couples eat supper in the back yard under festive Japanese lanterns, but the child is too disgusted to participate: " 'I ain't eating with them,' the child said and snatched her plate off the table and carried it to the kitchen and sat down with the thin blue-gummed cook and ate her supper. 'Howcome you be so ugly sometime?' the cook asked. 'Those stupid idiots,' the child said."

And then—for who, given such details as these, can keep from seeing this story as a portrait of the artist as a young girl?—what are we to make of the passage that follows? It is one of several passages in the story that make the dim suggestion that the child would, in a way, like to be part of that scene she constantly lambastes if she could, if she were not so fundamentally unable to see pitilessly through to the banal and absurd: "The lanterns gilded the leaves of the trees orange on the level where they hung and above them was black-green and below them were different dim muted colors that made the girls sitting at the table look prettier than they were. From time to time, the child turned her head and glared out the kitchen window at the scene below." The cook says, tuning up another phrase—"God could strike you"—of what the reader does not yet know will be the animating line of the story: "God could strike you deaf dumb and blind . . . and then you wouldn't be as smart as you is." "I would still be smarter than some," the child replies. Surely we are getting a glimpse of the origins in O'Connor's mind as a child of the whole mocked and blighted world of her fiction. What follows is the major episode of the story, in which the cousins return from the fair. But first O'Connor puts the child, and hence the reader, in the proper mood to respond to the words of the hermaphrodite. The narrator moves back to a track of the story laid down in the lunch scene, where we first discovered the child's private religious feelings through her secret fascination with the image of the temple of the holy ghost. These two crucial strains of the child's mind—her private unexpressed religiosity and her vigorously, indeed bombastically expressed sense of the banal and the absurd—have not yet grown together as they were to do, in effect, later on, producing the fierce prophetic narrator of the O'Connor fiction. (But of course we must account for the narrator of *this* story too.) The early paragraphs of this scene are, for good or ill, among O'Connor's most poetic paragraphs; on the whole, I think, for good—observe, for instance, the startling image at the end of this first paragraph:

> After supper they left for the fair. She wanted to go to the fair but not with them so even if they had asked her she wouldn't have gone. She went upstairs and paced the long bedroom with her hands locked together behind her back and her head thrust forward and an expression, fierce and dreamy both, on her face. She didn't turn on the electric light but let the darkness collect and make the room smaller and more private. At regular intervals a light crossed the open window and threw shadows on the wall. She stopped and stood looking out over the dark slopes, past where the pond glinted silver, past the wall of woods to the speckled sky where a long finger of light was revolving up and around and away, searching the air as if it were hunting for the lost sun. It was the beacon light from the fair.

The child associates somehow her own visits to the fair in years past with her early desire to be a doctor and later an engineer. Tonight, however, she feels that "she would have to be much more than just a doctor or an engineer: she would have to be a saint."

She would have to be a saint because that was the occupation that included everything you could know; and yet she knew she would never be a saint. She did not steal or murder but she was a born liar and slothful and she sassed her mother and was deliberately ugly to almost everybody. She was eaten up also with the sin of Pride, the worst one. She made fun of the Baptist preacher who came to the school at commencement to give the devotional. She would pull down her mouth and hold her forehead as if she were in agony and groan, "Fawther, we thank Thee," exactly the way he did and she had been told many times not to do it. She could never be a saint, but she thought she could be a martyr if they killed her quick.

And her fantasy is of her martyrdom—a fantasy such as children used to have, one guesses, in times gone by, but surely a peculiar one today; she imagines her death at the hands of the Romans, but there is a slightly comical touch: they try to burn her but she won't "burn down," and finally they cut off her head and she goes immediately to heaven. The child says her prayers, and we are told that though "they were usually perfunctory," that "sometimes when she had done something wrong or heard music or lost something, or sometimes for no reason at all, she would be moved to fervor and would think of Christ on the long journey to Calvary, crushed three times under the rough cross." But notice how even in this relatively tender scene O'Connor cuts through the threatening piety and emotionalism by framing the lines just quoted with these two details: first, that the child, on the verge of her prayers, is trying to think of "something cold and clammy" to put in her cousins' bed and second, that the reason for the fervor of her prayers tonight is that she thinks of the farm boys who are escorting her cousins: "Tonight, remembering Wendell and Cory, she was filled with thanksgiving and almost weeping with delight, she said, 'Lord, Lord, thank You that I'm not in the Church of God, thank you Lord, thank You!' and she got back in bed and kept repeating it until she went to sleep."

When the cousins return giggling from the fair, the child wakes up and hears one say to the other: "I enjoyed it all but the you-know-what," and the child, rabid to know what this is, is not in too repentant a mood to think up another lie to pry the story out of them—if they will tell her about what they saw at the fair, she'll tell them about the time she saw a rabbit having babies. And this is what the cousins saw and heard:

> It had been a freak with a particular name but they couldn't remember the name. The tent where it was had been divided into two parts by a black curtain, one side for men and one for women. The freak went from one side to the other, talking first to the men and then to the women, but everyone could hear. The stage ran all the way across the front. The girls heard the freak say to the men, "I'm going to show you this and if you laugh, God may strike you the same way." The freak had a country voice, slow and nasal and neither high nor low, just flat. "God made me thisaway and if you laugh He may strike you the same way. This is the way He wanted me to be and I ain't disputing His way. I'm showing you because I got to make the best of it. I expect you to act like ladies and gentlemen. I never done it to myself nor had a thing to do with it but I'm making the best of it. I don't dispute hit." Then there was a long silence on the other side of the tent and finally the freak left the men and came over onto the women's side and said the same thing.
>
> The child felt every muscle strained as if she were hearing the answer to a riddle that was more puzzling than the riddle itself. "You mean it had two heads?" she said.
>
> "No," Susan said, "it was a man and woman both. It pulled up its dress and showed us. It had on a blue dress."
>
> The child wanted to ask how it could be a man and woman both without two heads but she did not. She wanted to get back into her own bed and think it out and she began to climb down off the footboard.

Thus set before the child, the crucial lines couched in the lowly patois of the wretched Negro hermaphrodite, is a double mystery: the mystery of God's unfathomable will for men—*This is the way he wanted me to be*—and the almost greater mystery of the power of the afflicted believer to accept God's will on simple faith.

But what has all this exactly to do with the rest of the story? If this is the climactic scene, harmonizing everything that has gone before, what about all the business about the temple of the Holy Ghost? And what is the child's real reaction to the freak's peculiar affliction anyway? And here one supposes that the narrator might have told us something like this: "And the child, reflecting on the strange, thrilling words of the freak, thought about what the sister had told her cousins to say when boys made advances to them in the back of an automobile: 'Stop sir, I'm a temple of the Holy Ghost!' And she reflected that not only her cousins, herself, and poor Miss Kirby, but even this miserably defective creature as well, was a child of God and a temple of the Holy Ghost." But of course this is not at all what the narrator does—she creates this delicate, rhythmic, incantatory reverie, infinitely more expressive of the child's secret awe:

> She lay in bed trying to picture the tent with the freak walking from side to side but she was too sleepy to figure it out. She was better able to see the faces of the country people watching, the men more solemn than they were in church, and the women stern and polite, with painted-looking eyes, standing as if they were waiting for the first note of the piano to begin the hymn. She could hear the freak saying, "God made me thisaway and I don't dispute hit," and the people saying, "Amen. Amen."
> "God done this to me and I praise Him."
> "Amen. Amen."
> "He could strike you thisaway."
> "Amen. Amen."
> "But he has not."
> "Amen."
> "Raise yourself up. A temple of the Holy Ghost. You! You are God's temple, don't you know? Don't you know? God's Spirit has a dwelling in you, don't you know?"
> "Amen. Amen."
> "If anybody desecrates the temple of God, God will bring

him to ruin and if you laugh, He may strike you thisaway.
A temple of God is a holy thing. Amen. Amen."
"I am a temple of the Holy Ghost."
"Amen."
The people began to slap their hands without making a
loud noise and with a regular beat between the Amens,
more and more softly, as if they knew there was a child
near, half asleep.

The story is lowered to its conclusion from this dreamy
height by a brief description of the cousins' return to the
convent the next day. The mother and the cousins con-
verse in the back seat of the car, but the child will not
listen to any of this "twaddle" and maintains her position
outside these banal affairs by sitting in the front seat close
to the door and comically holding her head out of the window. At the convent the child mentally castigates the
whole place, declines to be embraced by the nuns, and
about the benediction they are just in time to attend, she
thinks, "You put your foot in their door and they got you
praying." But in the chapel, when the Host is raised, her
thoughts fly again to the words of the hermaphrodite: "I
don't dispute hit. This is the way He wanted me to be."

On the way home the child amuses herself by observing
the fat folds of flesh in the neck of the boy driving them,
and his pig-like ears; and it is this character who makes
possible the small ironical turn that clicks the story shut.
The mother asks the boy if he has been to the fair and
he says that he has and that it was a good thing that he
went when he did because it has just been shut down.
"Some of the preachers from town gone out and inspected
it and got the police to shut it on down." We know no more
than this, nor do we know exactly what the child is thinking about what she has heard, except that "her round face
was lost in thought" and that—in the brief lyrical rise
that O'Connor often uses to close her stories—her mind
is stirred to create, from the sight of the sun sinking behind the trees, another Christian image: "She turned it
[her face] toward the window and looked out over a

stretch of pasture land that rose and fell with a gathering greenness until it touched the dark woods. The sun was a huge red ball like an elevated Host drenched in blood and when it sank out of sight, it left a line in the sky like a red clay road hanging over the trees."

"A Temple of the Holy Ghost," in its benign and even tonality, stands at the opposite pole from such a formidable story as "A Good Man Is Hard to Find." In "A Temple of the Holy Ghost" the reader rides smoothly through on the tide of his quickly engendered and never seriously threatened sympathy for the child—for her sincerity and sensitivity and her clever wit. Like all the children of the widow-child stories, she is also sullen and egotistical, but an important difference between her and the others is that she has the faculty of self-criticism. In general O'Connor liked to take for her subjects in the short stories people who lacked this faculty and build her drama around the sudden collapse of their coddled views of themselves. The arrogant, self-pitying Asbury in "The Enduring Chill," for instance, cannot believe his ears when the priest says, "The Holy Ghost will not come until you see yourself as you are—a lazy, ignorant conceited youth!"

A story that also describes a hard lesson in humility for the protagonist but which is tonally much closer to "A Temple of the Holy Ghost" is "The Artificial Nigger." Mr. Head is a believer, a true Christian, and therefore, like the child in "A Temple of the Holy Ghost" and all other religious characters in O'Connor, basically good and right; any sins of his, we can be sure, are going to be quite indulgently dealt with, *his* lesson in humility quite tenderly viewed. Here is the final scene of the story, showing Mr. Head and his grandson Nelson returning home safely at last from their terrifying visit to the city, where they have both behaved quite shamefully—Mr. Head by denying, in his fear of a hostile crowd, that Nelson was his grandson, and Nelson by withholding from his grandfather his forgiveness:

Their train glided into the suburb stop just as they reached the station and they boarded it together, and ten minutes before it was due to arrive at the junction, they went to the door and stood ready to jump off if it did not stop; but it did, just as the moon, restored to its full splendor, sprang from a cloud and flooded the clearing with light. As they stepped off, the sage grass was shivering gently in shades of silver and the clinkers under their feet glittered with a fresh black light. The treetops, fencing the junction like the protecting walls of a garden, were darker than the sky which was hung with gigantic white clouds illuminated like lanterns.

Mr. Head stood very still and felt the action of mercy touch him again but this time he knew that there were no words in the world that could name it. He understood that it grew out of agony, which is not denied to any man and which is given in strange ways to children. He understood it was all a man could carry into death to give his Maker and he suddenly burned with shame that he had so little of it to take with him. He stood appalled, judging himself with the thoroughness of God, while the action of mercy covered his pride like a flame and consumed it. He had never thought himself a great sinner before but he saw now that his true depravity had been hidden from him lest it cause him despair. He realized that he was forgiven for sins from the beginning of time, when he had conceived in his own heart the sin of Adam, until the present, when he had denied poor Nelson. He saw that no sin was too monstrous for him to claim as his own, and since God loved in proportion as He forgave, he felt ready at that instant to enter Paradise.

Nelson, composing his expression under the shadow of his hat brim, watched him with a mixture of fatigue and suspicion, but as the train glided past them and disappeared like a frightened serpent into the woods, even his face lightened and he muttered, "I'm glad I've went once, but I'll never go again!"

"The Artificial Nigger" is one of the more popular O'Connor stories; it has turned up in a number of texts and collections, and critics have not been slow to plumb its symbolical elements—to focus, for instance, on the fact that Mr. Head's denial of Nelson is made three times; but there are problems and implausibilities in this tale, it seems to me, that render it a somewhat less satisfactory story than "A Temple of the Holy Ghost." At the center of "The Artificial Nigger" is a device very similar to the use of the hermaphrodite in "A Temple of the Holy Ghost": the Heads's amazed encounter, that is, with a statue of a Negro seen in a yard as they walk along a city street trying to find their way back to the train station. The Heads apparently come from one of those middle Georgia counties where Negroes have been successfully kept out, where they have even been afraid of passing through; the boy has never seen a black man before his visit to the city, and neither he nor his uncle have ever seen an artificial one, that is, a statue of one. We are asked to believe that this statue embodies for them all the mystery and wonder, not only of the city (however wicked it may be) but of all God's works, and that the shock of this encounter is enough to bring them together in their common humility and awe: "They could both feel it dissolving their differences like an action of mercy." But this incident seems too frail to bear so much of the story's meaning. How much more natural and plausible is the child's reaction to the curious words of the hermaphrodite in "A Temple of the Holy Ghost."

But one word more may be said about "A Temple of the Holy Ghost" before we move on to another story. The concentration on the interior drama in this story links it, like other qualities of the tale, to the mild early stories O'Connor wrote at Iowa. In the mature stories, though we always have considerable insight into the protagonists' minds, we also have highly colored conflict outside— O'Connor generally felt the need of a plot full of bizarre, vivid, and often violent incidents; she used such a plot even in the heavily psychological *The Violent Bear It Away*. At the time that O'Connor was writing *Wise Blood* she turned away, as we have seen, from inner drama; Fitzgerald writes that she said during this time about Harry's alleged drowning of his wife in *The Family Re-*

*union* that Harry had actually pushed his wife overboard. "If nothing happened, there's no story," Fitzgerald quotes her as saying.[3] In nearly everything she wrote after *Wise Blood* psychological drama is extremely important, but at its most intense it is usually a function of a calamitous change in the main character's external fortunes, as in the two stories, for instance—"Everything That Rises Must Converge" and "The Comforts of Home"—where a young man witnesses at the end his mother's sudden death.

But perhaps one need hardly repeat that conflict and calamity were the things that O'Connor stories thrived on. In many of the short stories the conflict is between the complacent protagonist and some dangerous, alien intruder—Mrs. May's bull, for instance, the Misfit, the Bible salesman in "Good Country People," the refugee farmhand in "The Displaced Person," and in the story we are about to examine, a devilish trio of youngsters from the city.

3

"A Circle in the Fire" is a richly entertaining story that as a simple tale is perfectly plausible and lifelike but which is vibrant from first to last with meaning. As in many fine stories, one may feel on first reading it quite satisfied with the suffused meaning of the tale, with what it suggests about human nature and human plight, without being at all embarrassed at not being able to say what exactly it does say or suggest. Pressed for a statement of its theme, we can do no better than this: Life is dangerous, no one is safe, we all live each day on the verge of misfortune. Nothing, of course, could be more self-evident, and yet this is a simple, terrible truth of eternal interest, said most expressively, perhaps, in the famous passage of Ecclesiastes:

3. Introduction to *Everything That Rises Must Converge*.

I returned, and saw under the sun, that the race is not to the swift, nor the battle to the strong, neither yet bread to the wise, nor yet riches to men of understanding, nor yet favour to men of skill; but time and chance happeneth to them all.

For man also knoweth not his time: as the fishes that are taken in an evil net, and as the birds that are caught in the snare; so are the sons of men snared in an evil time, when it falleth suddenly upon them. (Ecclesiastes 9: 11–12)

And certainly we have here a major theme—the changeableness of men's fortunes and the mutability of all earthly things—of the body of O'Connor's work, a theme in which, in her case, the simple idea "Life is dangerous, no one is safe" is resolved not with the lighthearted heathen imperative "Therefore seize the day" but with the other-worldly imperative of Christian resignation: "Therefore seek God, for only God is eternal." This theme of man's vulnerability—dominated by the idea simply of his mortality—always lies close to whatever story O'Connor is telling and is brought forward from time to time to dominate the reader's attention, as in the Ozymandias-like museum scene in *Wise Blood* where Enoch Emery, showing Hazel the shrunken mummy, says, "He was once as tall as me or you." A major difference in the appearance of this theme in O'Connor and in other modern writers is that the idea of man's vulnerability and his mortality is generally used in O'Connor more as a whip and scourge against him—much as it is used in southern tent evangelism—than as a just cause for our pity and sympathy; "A Circle in the Fire" is, as we shall see, somewhat less harsh in this respect than other O'Connor stories. We generally see the O'Connor protagonists as people who desperately need to be taught a lesson. In "Revelation," for instance, one of the stories in which the idea of human vulnerability is quite central, we see Mrs. Turpin, the very moment before she is struck on the head by the book hurled by the outraged girl in the waiting-room, mentally counting her many well-earned blessings:

"When I think who all I could have been besides myself and what all I got, a little of everything, and a good disposition besides, I just feel like shouting, 'Thank you, Jesus, for making everything the way it is.' " But from this moment on, things will not be "the way they are" for Mrs. Turpin again. Similarly, when at the end of "A Circle in the Fire" the three boys set fire to Mrs. Cope's precious woods, her nervous conviction that she can handle, can "cope with," whatever trouble comes her way—that she has, in a sense, o'ermastered fate and that misery will come to those who have not worked so hard or thanked God so much—is dealt a serious blow.

But in any case, one can argue that tonally speaking this story is perfectly brought off. Reading "A Circle in the Fire," one feels momentarily quite won over to that peculiar and original O'Connor tonality of which we have had so much to say and which comes more and more to appear, as we compare one story to another, to be both her main strength and her special weakness as a writer. "A Circle in the Fire" is laughing comedy of a very high order; it is intensely entertaining to witness the growing distraction of this nice Mrs. Cope, the victim in spite of everything—intensely funny to watch her being brought down in this particular way. In other words, there is here a heavy element of comic comeuppance. We foresee that something unpleasant will happen to Mrs. Cope in the end, we expect to enjoy it if it is not too severe, and it is not —that is an important point; still, when it comes it strikes deeper than we had expected it to; it darts unexpectedly through our comic defenses to draw us momentarily close, not only to Mrs. Cope, but to the others as well, in what we now see to be their common plight. Or to put it another way, one might say about Mrs. Cope that the slender threads of sympathy that have wound into our comic contempt for her during her ordeal with the boys are at the end pulled taut, and when her pain and humiliation comes, we find that—as funny, in a way, as it is—we are not in-

different to it. Because of the nature of the deft tonal
resolution at the end, which is in the direction of pity and
involvement, this tale is somewhat closer than most
O'Connor stories to the compassionate comedy of Faulkner, or, let us say, of Katherine Anne Porter (as in such
a delicately toned piece, for instance, as "Noon Wine");
yet the balance in "A Circle in the Fire" between serious
and comic elements is, as we shall see, still something
quite different from anything in Faulkner or Porter.

Besides "A Circle in the Fire" there are three other
O'Connor stories in which the idea of the insecurity of all
worldly successes and achievements clearly dominates,
and they are all in the widow-child series of tales: aside
from "Circle" and the above-mentioned "Revelation," we
have "The Displaced Person" and "Greenleaf." One can
certainly place "Revelation" along with "Circle" in the
innermost circle of O'Connor's best, but the latter two
stories are not nearly so satisfactory, and part of the
problem seems to lie in inadequate tonal resolutions at the
end. All of these stories give us cunningly comic pictures
of hard-working and energetic farm-women who are
proud of the good life they have made for themselves on
their well-ordered farms, who believe they have attained
their station in life by sheer strength of character, who
hold in enormous contempt everyone who has not arrived
where they have arrived, and who suddenly have this high
ground of well-being and success rather violently
wrenched from under them. It is not a mere coincidence,
probably, that it is the two lesser of these stories that
end in total or near-total catastrophe; Mrs. May dies on
the horns of the invading bull, and Mrs. McIntyre's health
is ruined and her farm lost as a result of the grotesque
accidental death of her emigrant farm-hand. In the other
two stories we assume that the outer life will go on for
the protagonists pretty much as usual, but that they have
suffered some severe inner shock.

A comment by Stanley Edgar Hyman might here be

interposed. Hyman said of O'Connor's last collection of short stories that he thought she had come to rely too much on death to end them[4]—his dissatisfaction with some of the more violent stories may stem from the fact that the devastating and painful conclusions to these pieces tend to throw finally out of its precarious balance the peculiar O'Connor tonality. Endings in short stories matter, after all, a good deal more than they do in novels and tend to color one's whole feeling about a tale much more than in the longer form. (One tends, in fact, to forget the endings of novels, even of those one knows best.) But in any case, to end a story, and particularly a satiric story, with (and therefore lay great stress on) untimely and painful death would tend to pose an unusual challenge for a writer with the very harsh and uncharitable religious views of O'Connor, for it is, after all, in conflicting attitudes toward death that the God-centered and the humanistic views are most deeply divided. The emotions that people in our age feel about death and therefore about death in art when it is at all realistically portrayed, are emotions that refuse to be fully circumscribed within O'Connor's tonal framework, emotions that tend to flood over the tonal boundaries of her work. (We virtually always look on death as sad and sorrowful; it presents itself to us much more as an end than as a beginning: we are not attuned to the idea—some of us consciously reject it altogether—that there is any regaining in a world to come the losses suffered in this one.) Obviously this is not *always* the case; in spite of whatever philosophical differences we may have with the teller of the death of Hazel Motes, we can enter into the spirit in which that death is told; but it is often a different matter in the short stories, where the protagonists are nearly always more harshly dealt with.

4. Hyman, *Flannery O'Connor*, 45.

I think one has to range far back into medieval literature to find tales that are tonally as formidable and difficult as are some of O'Connor's. There is a recent essay by
Morton Bloomfield which attempts to explain the reasons
for the modern reader's discomfort with the pathetic tales
of Chaucer—Bloomfield concentrates on the Man of Law's
Tale—and to see in what sense these tales are comedies
and in what sense they can be said to be tragedies, in
short to discover how in Chaucer's time they were meant
to be regarded and enjoyed. It was strange to turn to this
essay (attracted by its title: "The Man of Law's Tale: A
Tragedy of Victimization and a Christian Comedy") in a
recent issue of PMLA and after reading it to find that
one had overlooked its epigraph in small print at the beginning—it is a line from O'Connor's preface to *Wise
Blood*: "All comic novels that are any good must be about
matters of life and death." The essay itself does not mention O'Connor, but there is a passage describing the pathetic tales of Chaucer which seems extremely apropos to
the tonal dilemma in such O'Connor tales as "A Good Man
Is Hard to Find," "Greenleaf," and "The Displaced Person."

The source of our uneasiness with the pathetic tales is the
clash between the subject which demands involvement and
the style which continually pushes us to a distance. We are
prepared for comedy by the mode of writing but instead
read of tragic episodes. The hero or heroine is not a tragic
figure, nor a comic figure, but a victim. Our emotional response is thus contradictory. We cannot identify with the
protagonist as we long to do, because the author or persona
perpetually keeps us at a distance. . . . We cannot laugh
at the protagonist as the tone demands, because he undergoes such frightful experiences. This type of unresolved
clash between the comic and the tragic gives us what might
be termed the tragedy of the victim or a pathetic tale. The
tragedy of victimization is not a true tragedy because we
cannot identify ourselves emotionally with a protagonist we
perpetually feel superior to and whose sufferings create no

awe in us. We witness no mighty hero in his agony, but rather a hapless victim of circumstances whose fate verges on the funny.[5]

Now obviously the O'Connor stories are in many respects very different from the pathetic tales in Chaucer; for one thing, O'Connor's victims are much more satirically and contemptuously dealt with—they are not quite "hapless." Nevertheless, the nature of all these "Christian comedies," if that designation is to be used—it implies, of course, that they are not comedies in any ordinary sense of the term today—is quite similar; for the pathetic tales, if Bloomfield is right, appealed to a facet of the medieval mind that wanted and needed, being earnestly Christian, to learn to be dead to the world, to repudiate the world, to be able to look on all earthly experience, even the most painful, as absurd, ultimately unimportant, and therefore merely comic; and I think that many O'Connor stories are, among other things, an attempt to appeal to—or to engender—just such a mood. "The world must not be too much with us," Bloomfield writes, "in order to partake of Christian comedy after the tragedy of victimization." And in this statement lies, I think, a key to understanding our problem with the harsher O'Connor stories as well—though it does not necessarily make us think better of them. Consider, for instance, that what O'Connor succeeds in making funniest about her victims, even in the milder tales, is not so much their failings and defects—although these are funny enough—but simply their sense of involvement *per se.*

In "A Circle in the Fire," for instance—to move back into the story we have set out to discuss—O'Connor makes fun from the very beginning of Mrs. Cope's grim determination to protect her place. Even her weeding of the flower beds in the opening scene is funny: "She

5. Morton Bloomfield, "The Man of Law's Tale: A Tragedy of Victimization and a Christian Comedy," PMLA, LXXXVII (May, 1972), 384–85.

worked at the weeds and nut grass as if they were an
evil sent directly by the devil to destroy the place." And
right away we get a comic view (the passage quoted a
few pages back), from the vantage point of Mrs. Cope's
young daughter, of Mrs. Cope's worry about fire in her
woods.

Even in a story full of remarkable effects the handling
of the extended opening scene in which this passage is
set is still very impressive. Mrs. Cope is weeding her
border beds in the front yard and carrying on a desultory
conversation with Mrs. Pritchard, the wife of the hired
man. The child, from whose vantage point—when we are
aware of any vantage point at all—the story unfolds
(somewhat oddly, it seems, at first) watches dumbly
from an upstairs window. Mrs. Pritchard, vividly drawn
as a woman who thrives on calamity, is telling a macabre
story about the double funeral of a woman and her baby
—the baby had been conceived and delivered in an iron
lung; this is a story decidedly not to Mrs. Cope's taste,
and she keeps trying to move it into some brighter chan-
nel. "I don't see myself how she had it in it," Mrs. Pritchard says, and Mrs. Cope merely begins her litany of pious
thanksgiving, which we come to recognize, as the story
moves on, as her way of fending off evil spirits and evading the fundamental mystery and uncertainty of life:

> "Every day I say a prayer of thanksgiving," Mrs. Cope
> said. "Think of all we have. Lord," she said and sighed,
> "we have everything," and she looked around at her rich
> pastures and hills heavy with timber and shook her head
> as if it might all be a burden she was trying to shake off
> her back.
> Mrs. Pritchard studied the woods. "All I got is four absess
> teeth," she remarked.
> "Well, be thankful you don't have five," Mrs. Cope snapped
> and threw back a clump of grass. "We might all be de-
> stroyed by a hurricane. I can always find something to be
> thankful for."
> Mrs. Pritchard took up a hoe resting against the side of
> the house and struck lightly at a weed that had come up

between two bricks in the chimney. "I reckon you can," she said, her voice a little more nasal than usual with contempt.

"Why, think of all those poor Europeans," Mrs. Cope went on, "that they put in boxcars like cattle and rode all over Siberia. Lord," she said, "we ought to spend half our time on our knees."

Underneath this amusing and grotesquely banal conversation, the seeming casualness of this scene in the yard on a summer day, one feels, nevertheless, a ruthless concentration of effect; one senses that through this banal talk the crucial motifs of the story are being dimly sounded, not only because of the direction of the conversation itself—with its themes of trouble and safety— but because of the language with which the conversation is framed and adorned. Two adjectives, for instance, in the opening line of the story—"black" and "livid"— quietly do their work: "Sometimes the last line of trees was a solid gray blue wall a little darker than the sky but this afternoon it was almost black and behind it the sky was a livid glaring white." And the sense of something ominous gathering itself to descend is deepened a few paragraphs on when the child, gazing out her bedroom window, imagines that the sky is "pushing against the fortress wall [of trees], trying to break through," and again—if one may skip ahead for a moment—during an early episode with the boys in which Mrs. Cope, picking up a plate that the three have just emptied of her sandwiches (like young Tarwater's, their deeper hunger—and Mrs. Cope learns this only too late—will not be so easily assuaged), looks up at the sun going down in front of them, "almost on top of the tree line," and we get this remarkable image: "It was swollen and flame-colored and hung in a net of ragged cloud as if it might burn through any second and fall into the woods." Such imagery is always strategically placed in the story so as not to occupy the front edge of the reader's attention, not to seem to lead the story, but only to provide a suggestive

context. And the same thing is true of the language of
the narrator's asides about the two women. What exactly
do we make, for instance, of the opening description of
Mrs. Cope as having eyes that "seemed to be enlarging
all the time behind her glasses as if she were continually
being astonished"? or of the indirect suggestion that Mrs.
Pritchard is not only one who thrives on disaster but is,
in a way, a harbinger of it: "Mrs. Pritchard folded her
arms and gazed down the road as if she could easily
enough see all these fine hills flattened to nothing"?

The opening tableau—the two women in their positions
in the front yard, the child watching from the window—
is still in place (having been disturbed only by the return
of the Negroes, who for Mrs. Cope are as "destructive
and impersonal as the nut grass," but with whom she has
at least learned to cope) when the main action of the
story begins with the appearance of the three boys. The
entrance of the three boys onto this carefully prepared
ground is arranged in a sly, indeed a nearly perfect, way:
the first glimpse of them on the road—it's the child who
sees them first, from her higher perch—is juxtaposed
with Mrs. Cope's firm insistence to Mrs. Pritchard that
when trouble comes, she'll be ready:

> [Mrs. Cope] pointed the trowel up at Mrs. Pritchard and
> said, "I have the best kept place in the county and do you
> know why? Because I work. I've had to work to save this
> place and work to keep it." She emphasized each word with
> the trowel. "I don't let anything get ahead of me and I'm
> not always looking for trouble. I take it as it comes."
> "If it all come at oncet sometimes," Mrs. Pritchard began.
> "It doesn't all come at once," Mrs. Cope said sharply.
> The child could see over to where the dirt road joined the
> highway. She saw a pick-up truck stop at the gate and let
> off three boys who started walking up the pink dirt road.
> They walked single file, the middle one bent to the side
> carrying a black pig-shaped valise.
> "Well, if it ever did," Mrs. Pritchard said, "it wouldn't
> be nothing you could do but fling up your hands."
> Mrs. Cope didn't even answer this. Mrs. Pritchard folded

her arms and gazed down the road as if she could easily enough see all these fine hills flattened to nothing. She saw the three boys who had almost reached the front walk by now. "Lookit yonder," she said. "Who you reckon they are?"

The best comedy of the story resides in the encounters that follow between Mrs. Cope and her three uninvited guests. Powell, the middle boy, had lived on her farm as a small child and always dreamed of coming back to play. "My daddy he's daid now," Powell tells Mrs. Cope, and her reply is followed by one of the narrator's most cunningly suggestive asides: " 'Dead. Well I declare,' Mrs. Cope said as if death were always an unusual thing. 'What was Mr. Boyd's trouble?' " Mrs. Cope's first ploy is to be nice and friendly to the boys and hope they'll be on their way: " 'Well well,' she said, glancing at the suitcase, 'it's nice of you to stop and see me. I think that was real sweet of you.' " But the boys linger, she brings out her cokes and crackers, and the conversation deteriorates. When she says, "So you boys live in one of those nice new developments," one of the boys replies, "The only way you can tell your own is by smell." Powell, whose stare—one eye has "a slight cast to it"—seems to pinch Mrs. Cope like a pair of tongs, reveals the boys' plan to spend the night: "My uncle brought us this far on his pick-up truck and he's going to stop for us again in the morning," and we get, through the child, one of those vivid comic images that so abundantly enrich and adorn the O'Connor tales: "There was a moment in which she [Mrs. Cope] didn't say a thing and the child in the window thought: she's going to fly out of that chair and hit the tree."

At this point the story dissolves, as it were, into a series of delicately constructed little episodes in which the war between the lady and her three visitors is gradually escalated. The boys are told not to ride the horses, but they do anyway. They get into the dairy and drink out of the milk cans. They send everybody into a fright

by letting out the bull. They chunk stones at Mrs. Cope's
mailbox. And the more the pattern is repeated the funnier
it becomes—Mrs. Pritchard's unreluctant bringing of the
latest bad news, for instance, and Mrs. Cope's repeated
attempts to contain her mounting anxiety. Their prom-
ised leave-taking does not take place. When Mrs. Cope
says, "Why boys! I thought you were going to meet your
uncle," Powell says, "We ain't though," and the big boy
says, "We ain't bothering nothing of yours":

> He couldn't see the way her eyes enlarged but he could
> take note of the significant silence. After a minute she said
> in an altered voice, "Would you boys care for some break-
> fast?"
> "We got plenty of our own food," the big boy said. "We
> don't want nothing of yours."
> She kept her eyes on Powell. His thin white face seemed
> to confront but not actually to see her. "You boys know
> that I'm glad to have you," she said, "but I expect you to
> behave. I expect you to act like gentlemen."
> They stood there, each looking in a different direction, as
> if they were waiting for her to leave. "After all," she said
> in a suddenly high voice, "this is my place."
> The big boy made some ambiguous noise and they turned
> and walked off toward the barn, leaving her there with a
> shocked look as if she had had a searchlight thrown on her
> in the middle of the night.

The precise rendering of each of these small episodes,
combined with the power of such suggestive imagery as
we get in the last line of the passage above to lift the
story above the level of simple homely drama (without
such careful handling, the story might, after all, have
seemed quite trivial) is something that is familiar in all
O'Connor's best work. In her best stories she found nearly
perfect vehicles, in other words, for those desperate things
that she wanted to convey, and her meaning could be
deeply suffused in the tale itself. Here the reader need
not constantly ask himself "What does this mean, what
does that mean?" as I think he has to do in *Wise Blood*,
in the second half of *The Violent Bear It Away*, and in

the more mechanically symbolic tales such as "The Artificial Nigger," "The Enduring Chill"—with its implausible and ineffectual business regarding the bird-shaped stain on Asbury's ceiling—or even in "The Displaced Person," where the meaning that one feels obliged to attach to the emigrant farmhand (and without which the story does not really seem very expressive) does not rise naturally out of the action itself but has to be consciously guessed at and worried over.

In all respects the three invading boys of this story are brilliantly done. There is no point at which the narrator seems to be forcing a meaning on her story that it is not designed to contain. What we actually see of them is ordinary enough, but from their first appearance on there is about them just the right degree of ominousness, of mysterious threat, achieved, for instance, in the eerie appearance of Powell's unmatched eyes—"his gaze," we are told, "seemed to be coming from two directions at once as if it had them surrounded." We certainly do not need to see the boys as simple evil exactly, because for one thing it is not pure and simple evil by which Mrs. Cope is finally overcome; and in any case we are prone to feel that *in a sense*—and this is an enormously important qualifier in terms of our overall response to the story—Mrs. Cope deserves what happens to her. As in most of the conflicts on which O'Connor short stories are erected, our sympathies are not bent clearly towards one party or another, but there is a tendency here to side against Mrs. Cope with the boys. All they have come for initially, after all, is a few days' romp in the country, and Mrs. Cope's constant warnings about the violation of *her* woods, *her* place, is as annoying to us as to them. We sympathize when the youngest child says, behind her back, "Man, Gawd owns them woods and her too."

Finally Mrs. Cope warns the boys that if they aren't gone by the next morning, she will call the sheriff. Mrs. Pritchard makes her usual prediction of disaster, and that night Mrs. Cope and the child spend an anxious evening on the porch, not knowing where the boys are, more or less keeping guard. By ten o'clock nothing has happened, and Mrs. Cope begins her childlike incantation of thanksgiving, in which are drawn together a number of the disaster-linked associations threaded through the story: " 'They've gone,' Mrs. Cope said, 'poor things,' and she began to tell the child how much they had to be thankful for, for she said they might have had to live in a development themselves or they might have been Negroes or they might have been in iron lungs or they might have been Europeans ridden in boxcars like cattle, and she began a litany of her blessings in a stricken voice, that the child, straining her attention for a sudden shriek in the dark, didn't listen to."

Just before the high agitation of its conclusion, O'Connor creates a rather tense lull in the story in which she again focuses the eye of the tale momentarily on the wide screen of tree and sky against which the little drama on the Cope farm is being played (in O'Connor one always feels in this kind of distancing of the action a rebuke of the anthropocentric view). Then the focus moves to the child, who has been heretofore little more than a silent witness to what has taken place but who must be brought forth in preparation for the special role she is to play in the finale. The season is changing and Mrs. Cope, as usual at such times "almost frightened at her good fortune in escaping whatever it was that pursued her," turns her attention to her daughter and her frightful appearance. "Why do you have to look like an idiot? . . . Suppose company were to come?" The child, as sullen and hateful as all the other children of these much-put-upon O'Connor widows, says, "Just leave me be. I ain't you," and she goes off to the woods "as if she were stalking out an enemy, her head thrust forward and each hand gripped on a [toy] gun."

The ordeal of Mrs. Cope has already been mirrored in

a small way in the child. The child has generally been contemptuous of Mrs. Cope's nervous fears of the boys and in favor of a tough line with them. At one point she had descended from her observation post upstairs wanting to "get that big boy down and beat the daylight out of him," and we have also had a glimpse of her face, with a "furious outraged look on it," in the back seat of the car when the two women drive down to the siege of the mailbox.

In any case, during this final morning the girl goes into the woods to play a pretend game of rounding up outlaws (much like Ruller in the early story "The Capture"), and hidden from view in the brush, she spies the three boys playing in the water in the cow trough. The rhythm of the boys' play is here nicely caught, as is the sudden intense absorption of Powell with an idea beginning to form in his mind. "If this place was not here any more . . . you would never have to think of it again," he says. The largest boy, putting forth an idea that will be comically picked up in the final scene, says that if he had this place, he would build a parking lot on it. Powell takes something small from his pocket and for a minute the three sit looking at it; then they go into the woods and start setting their fires. The dazed child watches the fire take hold, amidst the boys' whoops, and suddenly all her toughness and anger gives way to terror. These are the final paragraphs of the story:

> She turned and tried to run across the field but her legs were too heavy and she stood there, weighted down with some new unplaced misery that she had never felt before. But finally she began to run.
> Mrs. Cope and Mrs. Pritchard were in the field behind the barn when Mrs. Cope saw smoke rising from the woods across the pasture. She shrieked and Mrs. Pritchard pointed up the road to where the child came loping heavily, screaming, "Mama, Mama, they're going to build a parking lot here!"
> Mrs. Cope began to scream for the Negroes while Mrs.

Pritchard, charged now, ran down the road shouting. Mr. Pritchard came out of the open end of the barn and the two Negroes stopped filling the manure spreader in the lot and started toward Mrs. Cope with their shovels. "Hurry, hurry!" she shouted. "Start throwing dirt on it!" They passed her almost without looking at her and headed off slowly across the field toward the smoke. She ran after them a little way, shrilling, "Hurry, hurry, don't you see it! Don't you see it!"

"It'll be there when we git there," Culver said and they thrust their shoulders forward a little and went on at the same pace.

The child came to a stop beside her mother and stared up at her face as if she had never seen it before. It was the face of the new misery she felt, but on her mother it looked old and it looked as if it might have belonged to anybody, a Negro or a European or to Powell himself. The child turned her head quickly, and past the Negroes' ambling figures she could see the column of smoke rising and widening unchecked inside the granite line of trees. She stood taut, listening, and could just catch in the distance a few wild shrieks of joy as if the prophets were dancing in the fiery furnace, in the circle the angel had cleared for them.

That the child does not stand outside this misery when it comes seems exactly the proper touch: for of course the point is that no one can remain a witness to the common plight. The harsh comic light shed over all the action thus far fades away here in the end, and what is made most vivid is simply the characters' pain—note the use here for the first time of the affective term "her mother" in place of "Mrs. Cope"—and one realizes, seeing the mother and child as they are at the end, fixed in their attitudes of panic and alarm, that the cords of sympathy, though stretched out through the story very thin, have not been completely cut.

And what about the final image, which helps to transform this tale of the rather ordinary treachery of three children into a legend of man's helplessness and vulnerability? The look of misery on Mrs. Cope's face might have been worn, we are told, by Powell himself; these

young intruders are not to be seen, finally, as alien and
"other," for again the point is that no one—not even
Powell—is safe. Yet at this moment they may also seem
to bear, like the three prophets Meshach, Shadrach, and
Abednego, who came forth unscathed from Nebuchad-
nezzar's fiery pit, a message from above to prideful, for-
getful man.[6]

In "A Circle in the Fire," as in all O'Connor's finest
stories—in "Judgement Day," for instance, in "A Temple
of the Holy Ghost," in the marvelous tale about the identical hats titled "Everything That Rises Must Converge,"
in "Parker's Back"—the palpable reality, the compelling
actuality, of the experience being described is such that
(regardless of where one may stand in regard to the
writer's religious theses) one must submit to it, one must
fall under its spell. This is not to say these best and most
expressive O'Connor stories are not, in many senses of
the term, "Christian" stories. Some of them—"A Temple
of the Holy Ghost," for instance, "The River," and
"Parker's Back"—have Christian experience as their subject; and nearly all of them, including "A Circle in the
Fire," can accommodate—but the point is they do not
really demand—thoroughgoing Christian interpretation.
These are tales which seem to have no quarrel to pick
with the reader, where because consent to the truth of
the experience portrayed is assumed, one might say, by
the writer, it is easily granted by the reader. In O'Connor's best work one has no sense that the story is being
sacrificed to the idea; no sense that, as in "A Good Man
Is Hard to Find," the idea is being sprung like a trap
in one's face at the end; no sense that, as in the lam-
entably unconvincing and argumentative "The Lame
Shall Enter First," the action is a thin pretext for the
stubborn projection of some entirely resistible Christian
idea. For of course even where the action is a pretext, as

6. The story is told in Chapter Three of the Book of Daniel.

in a way it always is (one does not wish to portray the writer as struggling against, in the name of art, her desire to communicate her Christian view of life), the fact is that it must not seem to be. One ought to be able to feel that regardless of what idea, what doctrine about or vision of life, may lie behind or inspire the telling of thus and such a story, that the story is truly told, with due regard for the feeling about life that all of us, regardless of belief, share.

Readers of O'Connor, one finds, tend to be quite unimpressed with comparisons of this very odd American writer and D. H. Lawrence—how compare her ascetic, niggardly sentences, her grim religiosity and sneering comedy with Lawrence's passion and lyricism? But anyone who doubts that O'Connor and Lawrence were, in certain fundamental respects, very much the same kind of writer, writers with great natural gifts for narrative but with heavy evangelical impulses that could work frightfully against them, need only have recourse to David Daiches' chapters on Lawrence in his *The Novel and the Modern World*. Over and over again Daiches gives expression, in his assessment of Lawrence, to those very doubts and misgivings, and the frequent deep satisfactions, that form the experience of the O'Connor reader as well. Daiches insists that the "strong individual vision" that pervades all Lawrence's work was both his great strength and his weakness and accounts for both the "moving, even disturbing, persuasiveness" of his best work and the falseness and unreasonableness of his poorer, as well for the fact that his short stories—where the experience described must, one might say, be made to speak for itself—are better than his novels. "And if it is objected," Daiches writes, "that of course every novelist draws on his own experience, embodies his own view of the world, presents a vision derived from the way life has worked for him, that this is inevitable and by no means peculiar to Lawrence, we must still insist that in Lawrence the element of personal conviction, the suggestion that a given story is patterned so as to be able to hold something intensely, even defiantly, felt by the author, is found in Lawrence in a way that is not found in other great novelists." [7] And further on in the same passage Daiches has this to say: "In the short stories we feel that the action either contains what Lawrence wants to say, or it doesn't. There is rarely an approximation to success: the stories fail where the narrative is too crudely symbolic or where a meaning is imposed on the narrative by twists in the action or the dialogue that do not convince, and they succeed where the very texture of the narrative weaves as it moves the embodied meaning that Lawrence was seeking to communicate." And are not all these things largely true of O'Connor as well?

### 4

This study can perhaps best be brought to a close with an assessment of an O'Connor story quite different from the two widow-child tales we have been discussing. Nearly all of O'Connor's stories touch, in one way or another, on the lives of primitive, dirt-poor country people—in the widow-child stories, for instance, the hired help often have important parts to play—but in only a few of the stories are such people featured as they are in the novels; there is, for instance, the Misfit in "A Good Man Is Hard to Find," old Tanner in "Judgement Day," Mr. Shiftlet in "The Life You Save May Be Your Own," and Mr. Head and his grandson in "The Artificial Nigger"; but probably the lowliest of these low-life characters—the one most ignorant, that is, in the ways of the world—is O. E. (Obadiah Elihue) Parker of "Parker's Back."

"Parker's Back" was O'Connor's last work (it appeared in *Esquire* the spring after her death in the summer of

7. David Daiches, *The Novel and the Modern World* (Chicago, 1960), 178–79.

1964), but in certain important respects it is rather more like her first work *Wise Blood* than anything she wrote in the interim. "Parker's Back" is a very similar story of low life which is at times breathlessly close to farce; but in the short story she achieves the delicately balanced tonality and subtle harmonizing of farcical and serious elements that had eluded her (except for the final scenes of Hazel's repentance and death) in *Wise Blood*. "Parker's Back" tells a sometimes hilarious tale about the desperate religious experience of a country boy much like Hazel Motes: Parker has a face of Christ tattooed on his back to please his Straight Gospel wife, and looking at the face in the tattoo-artist's book and then with double mirrors at its reproduction in flashing colors on his own back, Parker is himself caught in the cool embrace of Christ's all-demanding eyes. The feat here is simply the successful infusion of high religious seriousness into a vividly colored folk tale of almost tall-tale magnification.

"Parker's Back" is one of the stories that exists in manuscript in the papers given in 1972 to the Georgia College library by Regina O'Connor, the author's mother. One may say here that though it may well be worth some scholar's time to pore over all these manuscripts at some leisure (there is rather abundant manuscript for all of the four volumes except the second, which is represented by only a few stories), a selective examination of them does not reveal anything that is especially interesting or surprising about the way O'Connor worked. We know from her own testimony that she was a slow and meticulous worker, and here we see her constantly revising her sentences and working over and over individual scenes, rewriting and rearranging them and often cutting them down quite brutally. The Georgia College manuscripts show, for instance, that, just as one would expect, those swift, vivid openings that are so much admired in O'Connor did not come easily; there seemed to be much hunting and picking through early drafts of a tale to find the right moment with which to begin and then quite thorough rewriting of the rest of the material to fit the opening. "Parker's Back" had originally begun with the scene in which Parker meets his wife-to-be, Sarah Ruth, and shows her his tattoos; in the final version we flash back to that scene as Parker, married and about to be a father, sits in shame and disgust on his own doorstep while Sarah Ruth, an ugly woman with skin as tight as an onion and eyes as sharp as ice-picks (images that O'Connor salvaged, as I recall, from draft after draft), snaps her beans on the front porch. A more interesting manuscript history is that of "The Life You Save May Be Your Own," where a great deal of material about Mr. Shiftlet's early life was cut from the final version, and where there are two alternate endings; in one of these Shiftlet is foiled of his magnificent effort to get hold of the old woman's car when after the marriage Mrs. Carter simply deposits Shiftlet and Lucy Nell at the train station; and in the other Shiftlet, after abandoning Lucy Nell at the lunch counter as in the final version, returns home to a wife and four children in another town and forthwith smashes in pious outrage a television set—a work of the devil in his eyes—that they had acquired during his absence.

One might pause here to say, about the Georgia College papers, that the most interesting file they contain is the correspondence between O'Connor and her literary agent, Elizabeth McKee, which contains well over a hundred letters; the correspondence seems to be complete on O'Connor's side but noticeably incomplete on McKee's— it may be that while the agency could supply the letters of O'Connor, it had not always kept copies of its own. This correspondence reveals O'Connor as a quite skilled manager of her own career, with careful tracking, for instance, of her manuscripts from journal to journal and quite efficient (one is tempted to say "quite worldly") record-keeping regarding her earnings. Money was a constant, indeed almost a frantic, concern of O'Connor during the years between her graduate student days at Iowa and her return to Milledgeville—while she was writing *Wise Blood,* that is—and in fact she continued to worry over her small income (one does not know just how small, for royalty reports are not given here, though fees for stories and for subsidiary rights sometimes are) throughout her life. She said about one of her rewritings of the early "The Geranium" that she didn't want to go to the penitentiary for selling a story twice but that if she did she would like to get a good price for it. O'Connor was not very concerned about the fate of her manuscripts once they were sold. (Of the television drama made from "The Life You Save May Be Your Own," a ridiculous travesty in which Gene Kelly played Mr. Shiftlet, she said she had been able to stand the ordeal of watching it by concentrating on the price paid for it.) But she was, on the other hand, magnificently immune to criticism of or suggestions about works in progress—as purely uncommercial in what and how she chose to write as anyone could well be, and completely confident of her own judgment from the beginning. The McKee file—which is full of the quintessential O'Connor wit and rhetoric and therefore entertaining to read for its own sake—begins while O'Connor was writing *Wise Blood* and comes to a close about a month before her death and during the time that she was writing "Parker's Back."

O'Connor's fascination with the country culture of "Parker's Back" (and of such works as *The Violent Bear It Away* and "The Life You Save May Be Your Own") and the fact that this culture served her artistically as well as it did probably derived in part from the fact that it was the culture farthest removed from the life that she and her family led in small-town southern society. To this culture she stood, of course, not as a participant, but as a fascinated bystander; and close Milledgeville friends at the college tell how Miss O'Connor loved to give and receive tidings of this low religious life and how she seized on little items and anecdotes about country preachers, gospel singers, and such in the newspapers— even in the want ads and personals.[8] An amusing episode concerning O'Connor's title for her third and unfinished novel, *How the Heathens Rage,* comes to light in the McKee correspondence. Readers of the Atlanta papers, and perhaps other southern papers as well, are familiar with long, fundamentalist biblical explications printed under this title as paid advertisements by some person or group that always remains anonymous, and we learn in the McKee file that O'Connor was at one time worried about being sued for her use of this title and that it was for this reason that she changed "heathen" (as the word appears in the advertisement) to "heathens"—the latter term also happens, of course, to be more comical.

But anyone who reads the O'Connor fiction knows that it was not just the comedy of these religious fundamentalists that drew O'Connor to them. She believed— or perhaps she merely suspected—that what true Christian belief still exists is largely to be found among just these seemingly freakish people, that for them belief could still be, as she liked to put it, "a matter of life and death." And the method in "Parker's Back" is to play to the hilt the comedy of O. E. Parker's obsession with his tattoos and of his queer marriage, while at the same time charging it all with religious meaning. We are four or five pages into the story of this clownish Parker before we begin to realize that there is going to be put forth

8. For many firsthand details concerning Miss O'Connor's later life in Milledgeville, I am indebted to James and Mary Barbara Tate, who were regular visitors to the O'Connor farm for many years. James Tate has placed on file with the O'Connor papers at Georgia College an interesting account of his conversations with Miss O'Connor at Andalusia.

I have also benefited from the reminiscences of a number of other Milledgeville acquaintances (I was an undergraduate at Georgia College from 1955 to 1958) who knew Miss O'Connor.

more than one way of looking at his odd behavior. A
turning point in the story comes, tonally speaking, with
this early passage about his enchantment with the tattooed man:

> Parker was fourteen when he saw a man in a fair, tattooed
> from head to foot. Except for his loins which were girded
> with a panther hide, the man's skin was patterned in what
> seemed from Parker's distance—he was near the back of
> the tent, standing on a bench—a single intricate design of
> brilliant color. The man, who was small and sturdy, moved
> about on the platform, flexing his muscles so that the
> arabesque of men and beasts and flowers on his skin ap-
> peared to have a subtle motion of its own. Parker was filled
> with emotion, lifted up as some people are when the flag
> passes. He was a boy whose mouth habitually hung open.
> He was heavy and earnest, as ordinary as a loaf of bread.
> When the show was over, he had remained standing on
> the bench, staring where the tattooed man had been, until
> the tent was almost empty.
> Parker had never before felt the least motion of wonder
> in himself. Until he saw the man at the fair, it did not enter
> his head that there was anything out of the ordinary about
> the fact that he existed. Even then it did not enter his
> head, but a peculiar unease settled in him. It was as if a
> blind boy had been turned so gently in a different direction
> that he did not know his destination had been changed.

It is the diction in the second paragraph—such a phrase
as "a blind boy . . . turned so gently"—that alerts us
to an unsuspected dimension in the story, and one can
hardly misjudge the spirit of this description, a few paragraphs on, of Parker in the navy: "He stayed in the
navy five years and seemed a natural part of the grey
mechanical ship, except for his eyes, which were the same
pale slate-color as the ocean and reflected the immense
spaces around him as if they were a microcosm of the
mysterious sea." But at the same time nothing of the
sublime banality of Parker's courtship of Sarah Ruth is
sacrificed:

> Parker had no intention of taking any basket of peaches
> back there [to Sarah Ruth's] but the next day he found

himself doing it. He and the girl had almost nothing to say
to each other. One thing he did say was, "I ain't got any
tattoo on my back."
"What you got on it?" the girl said.
"My shirt," Parker said. "Haw."
"Haw, haw," the girl said politely.

Much of Parker's comedy derives from the fact that,
like Enoch Emery in *Wise Blood,* he seems to be unable
to control his own actions and constantly finds himself
doing things he had not meant to do. He makes up his
mind to have nothing further to do with Sarah Ruth, but
the very next morning he finds himself in the County
Ordinary's office getting married. Then he finds that he
hates living with her but cannot leave her: "Every morning he decided he had had enough, and would not return
that night; every night he returned." All of this is a
terrible trial to Parker, and the one way that he can
relieve his consternation is to get more tattoos. His sense
that something is after him, is pushing him into decisions
for mysterious reasons of its own, reaches a climax when
he nearly kills himself by crashing his employer's tractor
into a tree. The image of his shoes, which had flown off
of him in the fiery crash, being eaten up by the fire comes
to signify for him his narrow escape from death and
drives him—along with his growing desire to please his
pious wife—to make a frantic trip to the city to fill up
the one remaining space on his body with some trans-
cendent tattoo: "Parker did not allow himself to think
on the way to the city. He only knew that there had been
a great change in his life, a leap forward into a worse
unknown, and that there was nothing he could do about
it. It was for all intents accomplished."
Now the point is that with all his tattoos Parker has
never been at all satisfied with the overall look of his
body: "The effect was not of one intricate arabesque of
colors but of something haphazard and botched." And

indeed the reader half-consciously realizes that this is a fair description of Parker's whole life—and, one might add, of all godless life as we see it in the O'Connor fiction. O'Connor's rendering of Parker's desperate sojourn in the city during the two days it takes to have his tattoo is done in such precise and expressive detail that Parker's strange compulsion, which when one stands back from the story may not look very plausible, is still made to seem quite real. There is, for instance, the scene in the Haven of Light Christian Mission where Parker puts on in his distraction his borrowed shoes to go to bed, and the wonderfully energetic account of his misadventure in the pool hall, where his friends jeer at his new tattoo.

Now this is not to say there are not, even in this vivid and generally compelling story, moments in which the reader may feel the story slipping, perhaps just perceptibly, from his grasp. I am referring to those moments where Parker is overcome with the religious emotion that finally, we are given to understand, opens his eyes to see that what matters in his life is not the design of his desperately adorned body, but of his neglected soul. Here is our view of Parker's mind just after he is thrown out of the pool hall:

> Parker sat for a long time on the ground in the alley behind the pool hall, examining his soul. He saw it as a spider web of facts and lies that was not at all important to him but which appeared to be necessary in spite of his opinion. The eyes that were now forever on his back were eyes to be obeyed. He was as certain of it as he had ever been of anything. Throughout his life, grumbling and sometimes cursing, often afraid, once in rapture, Parker had obeyed whatever instinct of this kind had come to him.

But what do we make of the line "The eyes that were now forever on his back were eyes to be obeyed"? One cannot always fully enter into Parker's religious experience, but is rather inclined to accept the fact of Parker's conversion as a "given," one might say, of the developing story and to feel that the real originality of the tale lies elsewhere—it lies in the richly entertaining and persuasive frame and context in which these mystical experiences are set. What makes this view possible is, once again, the relatively friendly and unmenacing tone of the story, for the reader does not have imposed on him the burden of having to say (at the height, perhaps, of some painful and violent scene) yes or no to an implied judgment on a character's religious decision and hence, as in such a story, for instance, as "A Good Man Is Hard to Find," to the whole rhetoric of the story.

As Parker returns home to Sarah Ruth, he is aware of a change in himself—"it was as if he were himself, driving into a new country though everything he saw was familiar to him, even at night." And when towards dawn he appears at his door and his wife, pretending not to know who he is, says, "Who's there?" Parker turns his head to the skies "as if he expected someone behind him to give him the answer." And here again, as so often in O'Connor, the natural world outside seems to interpose itself in the life within; a tree of light bursting over the skyline seems to Parker to illuminate at last his long ignored and abused soul and to show him—at least momentarily—the beauty within that he could not achieve without: "he felt the light pouring through him, turning his spider web soul into a perfect arabesque of colors, a garden of trees and birds and beasts."

But the story does not quite end on this plane of sober elevation. Here O'Connor's tonal instinct leads her to make exactly the right choice—to pitch the story downward again into a renewal of the robust comedy with which it began, and which for the reader is not any less funny for being now mingled with at least a dim sense of the intense significance of all these events for Parker himself. At the end we see poor Parker's hope of pleasing the fierce Sarah Ruth with his new tattoo cruelly thwarted:

> Trembling, Parker set about lighting the kerosene lamp. "What's the matter with you, wasting that kerosene this near daylight?" she demanded. "I ain't got to look at you."
>
> A yellow glow enveloped them. Parker put the match down and began to unbutton his shirt.
>
> "And you ain't going to have none of me this near morning," she said.
>
> "Shut your mouth," he said quietly. "Look at this and then I don't want to hear no more out of you." He removed the shirt and turned his back to her.
>
> "Another picture," Sarah Ruth growled. "I might have known you was off after putting some more trash on yourself."
>
> Parker's knees went hollow under him. He wheeled around and cried, "Look at it! Don't just say that! *Look* at it!"
>
> "I done looked," she said.
>
> "Don't you know who it is?" he cried in anguish.
>
> "No, who is it?" Sarah Ruth said. "It ain't anybody I know."
>
> "It's him," Parker said.
>
> "Him who?"
>
> "God!" Parker cried.
>
> "God? God don't look like that!"
>
> "What do you know how he looks?" Parker moaned. "You ain't seen him."
>
> "He don't *look*," Sarah Ruth said. "He's a spirit. No man shall see his face."
>
> "Aw listen," Parker groaned, "this is just a picture of him."
>
> "Idolatry!" Sarah Ruth screamed. "Idolatry! Enflaming yourself with idols under every green tree! I can put up with lies and vanity but I don't want no idolator in this house!" and she grabbed up the broom and began to thrash him across the shoulders with it.

The story's final image, of Parker weeping against the tree, is, in a way, a fitting one to have brought O'Connor's work to a close, for it is an image that nearly perfectly epitomizes the peculiar tension between high comedy and high religious seriousness which—when it is right—is perhaps the main fascination of her work:

> Parker was too stunned to resist. He sat there and let her beat him until she had nearly knocked him senseless and large welts had formed on the face of the tattooed Christ. Then he staggered up and made for the door.
>
> She stamped the broom two or three times on the floor and went to the window and shook it out to get the taint of him off it. Still gripping it, she looked toward the pecan tree and her eyes hardened still more. There he was—who called himself Obadiah Elihue—leaning against the tree, crying like a baby.

# Bibliography

At the present time one need not be overzealous in tracing one's own path through O'Connor materials, thanks to the careful labors of a number of devoted O'Connor students who have made the essential tools for study of her work available in a few convenient volumes. Aside from the four original O'Connor books (*Wise Blood*, Harcourt, Brace, 1952; *A Good Man Is Hard to Find and Other Stories*, Harcourt, Brace, 1955; *The Violent Bear It Away*, Farrar, Straus, and Cudahy, 1960; and *Everything That Rises Must Converge*, Farrar, Straus, and Giroux, 1965), the following three books are indispensable:

*The Added Dimension*, a compendium of O'Connor materials edited by Melvin J. Friedman and Lewis A. Lawson. This contains ten critical articles on O'Connor; interesting correspondence between O'Connor and William Sessions; a long collection of well-chosen samplings of O'Connor's statements about her writing from her essays, speeches, and interviews; and a number of enormously helpful bibliographies. Among the latter, a listing of the separate publications of all O'Connor's stories and chapters of novels is particularly useful for being given in order of publication. Book editions in all countries are also given in chronological order in a separate list. There is an extremely convenient and comprehensive list of book reviews for each of the four O'Connor books. And finally there is a thorough bibliography of critical articles on O'Connor, which of course now has to be supplemented by standard general bibliographies for the years since the appearance of *The Added Dimension* in 1966.

*The Complete Stories*, brought out by Farrar, Straus, and Giroux in 1971. The title is somewhat misleading in that four of the pieces included are excerpts of the two novels in very nearly the same form as the novel editions themselves. But it is good to have all the short stories between the covers of one book and particularly to have easy access to the seven short stories that had not been included in the two original collections; six of these (three had never been published anywhere before) are stories that O'Connor submitted for her master's thesis at the University of Iowa. Also included is the brief published excerpt from her third novel, "Why Do the Heathens Rage?"

*Mystery and Manners* (New York: Farrar, Straus, and Giroux, 1969), in which Robert and Sally Fitzgerald brought together most of the important non-fictional writings of O'Connor over the years. These include articles O'Connor wrote for journals such as *America, Esprit* (University of Scranton), and *Esquire* (her essay on peacocks) and contributions to books other than her own, as well as new material which the Fitzgeralds culled from her unpublished papers and speeches. I have not separately listed below the O'Connor non-fictional writings that are available in *Mystery and Manners.*

As for critical studies on O'Connor, there are now a great many in both article and book length; I have listed in the bibliography below only the ones I have cited in the text or to which I owe some special debt. For a beginner in O'Connor study, a monograph by Robert Drake (*Flannery O'Connor,* William B. Eerdmans, 1966) remains perhaps the best short introduction. A recent book by Sister Kathleen Feeley, who made a study of the books in Miss O'Connor's library, is an adequate guide to the religious backgrounds of O'Connor's thought: *Flannery O'Connor: Voice of the Peacock* (New Brunswick: Rutgers University Press, 1972).

As for writings on O'Connor's life, an essay by Robert Fitzgerald written as an introduction to *Everything That Rises Must Converge* is especially revealing. Many short reminiscences have found their way into print; a number of these (as well as a great many short tributes to O'Connor from well-known writers and scholars) are included in the special issue of *Esprit,* VIII (Winter, 1964), brought out as a memorial to O'Connor at the time of her death. O'Connor's letters have yet to be collected. Aside from the Sessions correspondence mentioned above, one might mention a long unpublished correspondence with Elizabeth McKee, O'Connor's literary agent, on file with the O'Connor papers at Georgia College library, Milledgeville, Georgia. About the Georgia College papers, one may also say that they consist primarily of O'Connor manuscripts for her four published books, although there is also a collection in the library of O'Connor memorabilia and of incidental notices in newspapers.

SOURCES

Abels, Cyrilly, and Margarita G. Smith, eds. *Best Stories from Mademoiselle.* New York: Harper, 1961.

Bernanos, George. *The Last Essays of Bernanos.* Translated by Joan and Barry Ulanov. Chicago: H. Regnery, 1955.

————. *The Star of Satan.* Translated by Pamela Morris. Paris, 1926.

Bloomfield, Morton. "The Man of Law's Tale: A Tragedy of Victimization and a Christian Comedy." *PMLA,* LXXXVII (May, 1972), 384–85.

Booth, Wayne C. *The Rhetoric of Fiction.* Chicago: University of Chicago Press, 1961.

Charles, Gerda. "Review of *The Violent Bear It Away.*" *New Statesman,* LX (September 24, 1960), 445–46.

Claudel, Paul and André Gide. *The Correspondence between Paul Claudel and André Gide.* Translated by John Russell, with introduction and notes by Robert Mallet. New York: Pantheon Books, 1952.

Cole, Marley. *Jehovah's Witnesses.* New York: Vantage Press, 1955.

Daiches, David. *The Novel and the Modern World.* Chicago: University of Chicago Press, 1960.

DeVitis, A. A. "The Catholic Novelist: Graham Greene and François Mauriac," in Robert C. Evans, ed. *Graham Greene: Some Critical Considerations.* Lexington, 1963.

Dostoevsky, Feodor. *Crime and Punishment.* Translated by George Gibian. New York: Norton Critical Editions, 1964.

Drake, Robert. *Flannery O'Connor.* Grand Rapids, Mich.: William B. Eerdmans, 1966.

Du Bos, Charles. *François Mauriac et le problème du romancier catholique.* Paris, 1933.

Eliot, T. S. *Selected Essays* (especially "Baudelaire" and "Religion and Literature"). New York: Random House, 1950.

————. *The Family Reunion.* London, 1939.

Esty, William. "In America, Intellectual Bomb Shelters." *Commonweal,* LXVII (March 7, 1958), 586–88.

Feeley, Sister Kathleen. *Flannery O'Connor: Voice of the Peacock.* New Brunswick: Rutgers University Press, 1972.

Fitzgerald, Robert. Introduction to *Everything That Rises Must Converge.* New York: Farrar, Straus, and Giroux, 1965.

———. "The Countryside and the True Country." *Sewanee Review,* LXX (Summer, 1962), 388–94.

Fugin, Katherine, Faye Rivard, and Margaret Sieh. "An Interview with Flannery O'Connor." *Censer* [College of St. Teresa, Winona, Minnesota], Fall, 1960.

Gilman, Richard. "On Flannery O'Connor." *New York Review of Books,* August 21, 1969.

Goyen, William. "Unending Vengeance." *New York Times Book Review,* May 18, 1952, p. 4.

Greene, Graham. *Brighton Rock.* London, 1938.

———. *The Lost Childhood and Other Essays.* London: Eyre and Spottiswoode, 1951.

Hawks, John. "Flannery O'Connor's Devil." *Sewanee Review,* LXX (Summer, 1962), 397.

Hendin, Josephine. *The World of Flannery O'Connor.* Bloomington: Indiana University Press, 1970.

Hicks, Granville. "A Cold, Hard Look at Humankind." *Saturday Review,* XLVIII (May 29, 1965), 23–24.

———. "A Writer at Home with Her Heritage." *Saturday Review,* XLV (May 12, 1962), 22–23.

Hyman, Stanley Edgar. *Flannery O'Connor.* Minneapolis: University of Minnesota Pamphlets on American Writers, 1966.

"Jehovah's Name to Be Declared in All the Earth." *The Watchtower,* August 1, 1970, pp. 456–62.

LaFarge, Oliver. "Manic Gloom." *Saturday Review,* XXXV (May 24, 1952), 22–23.

Lewis, C. S. *The Allegory of Love.* New York: Oxford University Press, 1958.

Lewis, R. W. B. "Eccentrics' Pilgrimage." *Hudson Review,* VI (Spring, 1953), 144–50.

Lorch, Thomas. "Flannery O'Connor: Christian Allegorist." *Critique,* X, 69–80.

Mauriac, François. *Letters on Art and Literature.* Translated by Mario Pei. New York: Philosophical Library, 1953.

———. *Second Thoughts.* New York, 1961.

———. *Thérèse.* Translated by Gerard Hopkins. London, 1947.

Meaders, Margaret Inman. "Flannery O'Connor: Literary Witch." *Colorado Quarterly,* X (Spring, 1962), 377–86.

Mercier, Vivian. "Sex, Success, and Salvation." *Hudson Review,* XIII (Autumn, 1960), 449–56.

Mizener, Arthur. Review of *The Violent Bear It Away. Sewanee Review,* LXIX (Winter, 1961), 161–63.

Mullins, C. Ross. "Flannery O'Connor, an Interview." *Jubilee,* XI (June, 1963), 32–35.

Nolde, Sister M. Simon, O.S.B. *"The Violent Bear It Away:* A Study in Imagery." *Xavier University Studies,* I (Spring, 1961–62), 180–94.

O'Connor, Flannery. For most of O'Connor's own writings see introductory note above. The following are uncollected:

——. An interview at the College of St. Teresa. See above, Fugin, Rivard, and Sieh.

——. "The Novelist and Free Will." *Fresco* [University of Detroit publication], n.s., I (Winter, 1963), 100.

——. "The Role of the Catholic Novelist." *Greyfriar* [Siena College, Loudenville, New York], VII (1964), 10.

Porter, Katherine Anne. "Virginia Woolf" in *The Collected Essays.* New York: Delacorte Press, 1970.

Prescott, Orville. Review of *The Violent Bear It Away.* New York *Times,* February 24, 1960, p. 35.

Rosenfeld, Isaac. "To Win by Default." *New Republic,* CXXVII (July 7, 1952), 19.

Rubin, Louis D., Jr. "Flannery O'Connor and the Bible Belt," in Friedman and Lawson, eds., *The Added Dimension.* New York: Fordham University Press, 1966.

——. "Flannery O'Connor: A Note on Literary Fashions." *Critique,* II (Fall, 1958), 11–18.

Rubin, Louis D., Jr. and Robert C. Jacobs, eds. *South: Modern Southern Literature and Its Cultural Setting.* New York, 1961.

Sessions, William. "A Correspondence," in Friedman and Lawson, eds., *The Added Dimension.* New York: Fordham University Press, 1966.

Sherry, Gerard E. "An Interview with Flannery O'Connor." *Critic,* XXI (June–July, 1963), 29–31.

Stallings, Sylvia. "Flannery O'Connor: A New Shining Light Among Our Storytellers." *New York Herald Tribune Book Review,* June 5, 1955, p. 1.

Stephens, Martha. "Flannery O'Connor and the Sanctified Sinner Tradition." *Arizona Quarterly,* XXIV (Autumn, 1968), 223–39.

Tate, James. Unpublished six-page essay titled "An O'Connor Remembrance" in O'Connor papers in Georgia College library, Milledgeville, Georgia.

Teilhard de Chardin, Pierre. *The Divine Milieu.* New York: Harper and Row, 1960.

*Times Literary Supplement.* Anonymous review of *The Violent Bear It Away.* October 14, 1960, p. 666.

Trowbridge, Clinton. "The Symbolic Vision of Flannery O'Con-

nor: Pattern of Imagery in *The Violent Bear It Away."
Sewanee Review,* LXXVI (April–June, 1968), 298–318.
Turnell, Martin. *The Art of French Fiction.* London, 1959.
Warnke, Frank J. "A Vision Deep and Narrow." *New Republic,*
CXLII (March 14, 1960), 18.
Warnach, Walter. "Un homme de chrétienté," in *George Bernanos,* ed., A. Bequin. Paris, 1949.
Wells, Joel. "Off the Cuff." *Critic,* XXI (August–September,
1962), 4–5, 71–72.
Zabel, Morton Dauwen. *Craft and Character in Modern Fiction.* New York, 1957.

# Index

PROPERTY OF
BAKER COLLEGE
Owosso Campus

ACQUIRED BY
BAKER COLLEGE
1992